CONVERSION
TO ISLAM
Untouchables' Strategy for Protest in India

بِسْمِ اللَّهِ الرَّحْمَنِ الرَّحِيمِ

يَا أَيُّهَا النَّاسُ إِنَّا خَلَقْنَاكُم مِّن ذَكَرٍ وَأُنثَىٰ وَجَعَلْنَاكُمْ
شُعُوبًا وَقَبَائِلَ لِتَعَارَفُوا ۚ إِنَّ أَكْرَمَكُمْ عِندَ اللَّهِ أَتْقَاكُمْ
إِنَّ اللَّهَ عَلِيمٌ خَبِيرٌ

O mankind! We have created you from a male
and female, and set you up as peoples and tribes
so you may recognize one another. Verily, the
noblest of you in the sight of God is the best in
conduct. Behold, God is Aware, Informed.
(Translation of Quran 49:13)

CONVERSION TO ISLAM

Untouchables' Strategy for Protest in India

Abdul Malik Mujahid

Foreword by
Lloyd I. Rudolph
Susanne Hoeber Rudolph

Anima Books

LIBRARY OF CONGRESS
Library of Congress Cataloging-in-Publication Data

Mujahid, Abdul Malik.
    Conversion to Isalm: untouchables' strategy for protest in India/Abdul Malik Mujahid.
        p.   cm.
    Bibliography: p.
    Includes index.
    ISBN 0-89012-050-1
    1. Untouchables — India.   2. Muslim converts — India.
    3. Communalism — India.   4. India — Social conditions — 1947-
I. Title.
DS422.C3M82 1988
305.5'68—dc19   88-2445
                                                                            CIP

Printed in USA

In loving memory of my grandmother
Sakinah Bibi
Who, born an untouchable,
chose Islam as her way of life,
and remains in our heart.

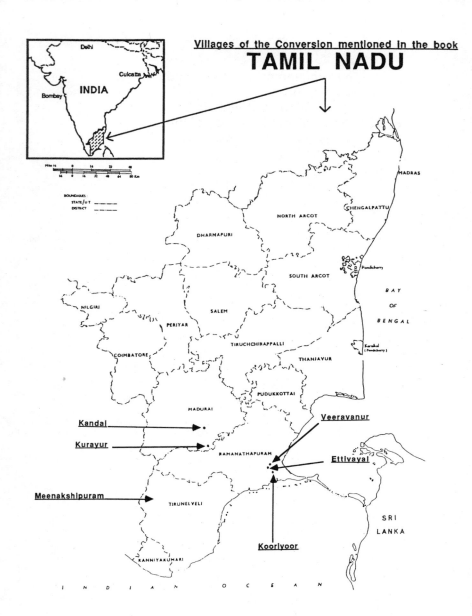

Villages of the Conversion mentioned in the book

TAMIL NADU

Contents

Foreword

Why did the conversion to Islam of several thousand South Indian untouchables in 1981-82 precipitate a Hindu resurgence in national politics? Why did the ex-untouchables in a few villages in and around Meenakshipuram in the Indian state of Tamil Nadu collectively attempt to abandon their local version of Hindu society by converting to Islam? What kind of people were they, and what were the experiences and expectations that led them to convert?

Abdul Malik addresses these questions in his penetrating and thought-provoking study. He places his inquiry and explanations of the events in and around Meenakshipuram in the larger regional and national contexts of Tamil Nadu's and India's history, society, politics, and theories of rebellious collective action. Much of value has been written about ex-untouchables, Muslims, and collective action in India, but no prior account brings these topics together in a common framework. It is in this sense that Malik's study is innovative as well as significant.

The untouchables in and around Meenakshipuram, Malik argues, had both negative and positive reasons for converting to Islam. Negatively, it was a rebellion against what they experienced as an obsolete and unjustified system of inequality. Positively, it was a means to realize the brotherhood and social status they believed Islam offered them as a religion and as a community.

We learn that ex-untouchables and Muslims in post-independence South India differ from ex-untouchables and Muslims in North India in ways that help to explain why the few conversions that have occurred took place in the south but not in the north. Islam in the south is a more attractive social identity than Islam in the north. In comparison with northerners, southern Muslims—some of whom have been associated for centuries with international and domestic trade and commerce—are more prosperous and better educated; do not suffer the ex-Mughal (ruler) complex that haunts their northern counterparts; did not lose their elites as a result of partition; speak and write in Tamil, the common language of the region, rather than in Urdu, the language of North Indian Muslims; and have played an active part in Tamil Nadu's politics of regional nationalism.

At the same time, ex-untouchables in the south are better treated and better-off than those in the north. Their rebellion through conversion in the south arose from frustration not misery, a central consideration in Malik's explanation of the conversions that did occur. Under Tamil Nadu's version of the policy of protective discrimination, ex-untouchables—dubbed ''scheduled castes'' in officialese—received better and more benefits and opportunities than ex-untouchables in most other states of the Indian Union. These include not only welfare payments, scholarships, and other forms of income transfer, places in government service, schools, and universities, but also lower levels of violence than in the states of North India where the police often aid or abet caste Hindu attacks and intimidation.

Because the benefits associated with protective discrimination for scheduled castes is confined to Hindus, the costs of rebellion through conversion to Islam include the loss of the privileges of backwardness. Indeed, there are those who argue that the policy of protective discrimination has been continued by ten-year intervals since independence in 1947 not only to provide recompense for past injustice and to promote social equality in the present but also to promote social control by making protest and rebellion through conversion so costly that scheduled caste ex-untouchables will not consider them.

There are also risks involved in protest. These were dramatically demonstrated in the first nationally noticed ''*Harijan* (untouchable) atrocity'' at Kilvenmani, Tamil Nadu, when in 1968 forty-two ex-untouchable landless laborers on strike for higher wages were confined in a hut and burned to death. Without minimizing the risks of protest and rebellion in Tamil Nadu, it remains true that atrocities since Kilvenmani have been much more common in the northern states of Bihar and Uttar Pradesh. Intimidation and violence as well as dependence, inequality, and misery are more pervasive and deep-rooted among ex-untouchables in North than in South India. Such considerations may help to explain why risk-averse ex-untouchables are more likely and more willing to protest and rebel in the South than in the North.

In Meenakshipuram and surrounding villages, Malik found that 80 percent of the population were ex-untouchables. Forty percent, well above the Indian average, were educated, and many were relatively well-off by village standards. Despite these "advances," they continued to be treated in ritual-rank terms as a race apart, barred not only from the contracting private space of caste Hindus' homes but also from the expanding public space of common facilities such as tea and barber shops and the front seats of buses.

The equality promised under India's constitutional guarantees was belied at the village level by the inability of caste Hindus of equal or lesser income and education to treat their ex-untouchable neighbors as fellow human beings. But as Muslims, former untouchables can enter both public and private space on an equal basis, not only drinking tea and having their hair cut but also eating with and marrying fellow Muslims. Malik's struggle with the prevailing theories and practice of caste in Islam provides an interesting and important insight into a disturbing but pervasive anomaly in Islamic practice.

Malik interprets conversion to Islam in the framework of concepts that Alexis de Tocqueville used to explain the French Revolution. Translated into contemporary social-science parlance, they are "rising expectations" and "relative deprivation." Conversion to Islam's brotherhood of equals becomes a way to achieve through collective action the equality and humanity denied them by the local version of Hinduism's social cosmology of ritual rank. Accepting Islam's beliefs and social cosmology by becoming a South Indian Muslim in Tamil Nadu denied the legitimacy of Hindu ritual cosmology and opened the way for ex-untouchables to realize a social status and human dignity commensurate with their secular and mundane circumstances.

Malik argues that a new kind of protest is abroad in India. It differs from earlier types of protest by caste or class movement—such as those by the Mahars in Maharashtra who converted to Buddhism, the Nadars of Madras and the Ezhavas of Kerala who formed caste associations to pursue social mobility and political power, or the untouchable landless laborers in the Thanjavur district of Madras who supported and voted for the Communist Party of India (CPI). By contrast, Malik portrays a type of resistance and rebellion which is scattered and parochial.

Heads of families in particular localities, rather than great leaders such as B.M. Ambedkar, Periyar E.V. Ramaswami Naicker, Guru Narainaswamy, or a political party such as the CPI, take the lead. Having become conscious of their own grievances and aspirations, heads of local families articulate them or act in ways that provide guidance or examples for neighbors in like circumstances. It is such parochial responses to the diffusion of new social conditions and ideas, not regional social movements or party mobilizations, that trigger and precipitate micro-level segmentary resistance, protest, and, sometimes, rebellion. Malik calls these leaders of hamlets or villages "little Ambedkars. . . . They feel more sharply and assert what they feel. Consequently," he adds, "the general atrocities increase in number."

Insofar as contemporary theories of collective or revolutionary action rely on organization and leadership or, minimally, diffusion of a common collective consciousness such as class, caste, or community, they lack concepts and language to account for the pattern of resistance, protest, and rebellion that Malik's account depicts. Because its cellular or segmentary form occurs in response to common social processes, it can be general even while, as a form of social action, it remains parochial. Unlike local resistance and rebellion in North India which usually generates a violent response (what the Indian press refers to as "atrocities against Harijans"), the conversions in Tamil Nadu were relatively nonviolent. By converting to Islam, the ex-untouchables in and around Meenakshipuram meant to commit a "hurt without shedding blood." Because the conversions were widely, some would say excessively, reported by the media, they became a national event. For some they became a national trauma. Indeed, the response from North India suggests that those who converted succeeded in ways they did not anticipate in committing a "hurt without shedding blood."

The conversions were depicted at the national level as a threat to Hinduism, an example for untouchables throughout the length and breadth of the land, whom defenders of Hinduism feared might be "ready" for rebellion through conversion to Islam. The "hurt" that the conversions inflicted led in part to introspection, self-criticism, and efforts to foster mobilization and political action that has continued up to the time these words are being written in September 1987.

The Meenakshipuram conversions triggered a trend that was deepened and accelerated by the constructions put on subsequent events such as Prime Minister Indira Gandhi's assassination in the context of Sikh terrorism and secessionism, the Shah Bano case* and the opening of the Ramjanmabhoomi Temple.** India's minorities, particularly Sikhs and Muslims, contributed to what M.J. Akbar has characterized as "the siege within," a sense on the part of those Hindus who equate their culture and history with India's that minorities who seek equality and who act to preserve and defend their social identity and interests somehow threaten national unity.

Trying to piece together an account of the circumstances and prospects of religious or caste communities in India is not an easy task. Official statistics purposefully shun publishing data that would make it possible to arrive at cross-tabulations of socio-economic variables. The government's policy is designed to avoid adding fuel to the fire of communal politics. But silence about the circumstances of religious communities and castes runs counter to another long-term policy commitment, protective discrimination, that provides social justice and promotes equality for "weaker sections," an official euphemism for poor, discriminated-against, and exploited minority communities.

Malik partially overcame these difficulties in his account of the relative prosperity of South Indian Muslims by using ingenious, unobtrusive and indirect measures based on newspaper advertisements of Eid to infer their relative socio-economic circumstances. His indefatigable and creative search for evidence fills in much of what official statistics fail to provide.

This searching book makes a major contribution to scholarship about religion and society. By carefully examining the local and regional causes and the national consequences of ex-untouchables' conversion to Islam in South India, Abdul Malik has deepened our understanding of the beliefs and actions associated with the pursuit of social justice and equality in India.

Lloyd I. Rudolph
Susanne Hoeber Rudolph
Landour, Mussoorie, UP

---

*A Supreme Court judgment in 1985 about Muslim personal law that led to a national soul-searching over the rights of the Muslim minority and of women as equal citizens.

**A 1985 lower court case that held that a historic building in Ayodhya claimed by Hindus to be Ram's birthplace and by Muslims to be a mosque established by Babar in the sixteenth century was a temple, not a mosque.

1

Introduction

Religion and caste are two dominant features of Indian society and politics. Forty years of a democratic, socialist, and secular constitution, ideology, and rhetoric have yet to have their meaningful impact on the political culture of the country. India in the eighties has witnessed an intensified communal competition and conflict. Such factors have always played a significant role in the history of India, but what makes the present case more complex is that although the demands, reasons, and causes of the ongoing "undeclared civil wars"[1] of India are mainly socio-economic, the social bases of the major actors and their lines of mobilization are religious and caste identities.

This book is about the assertive untouchables of India, who are participants in this ongoing violent phase of Indian society. Conversions are seen as one of the manifestations of aggressive behavior among untouchables. This book is, therefore, not a study in religion or history per se, as most of the classical studies of the religious conversions are, nor is it part of that social science literature which views conversion as a fantasy solution to stress situations.[2] It is rather a study of the complex social matrix in which some untouchables used conversion as a conscious and articulate protest against an unjust order.

The conversions being studied here were a more subtle form of aggression than physical violence. They evoked more bodily reaction and psychological response by the Hindu community they left than any other instance of clashes involving the same groups. In the Indian cultural context, this "psychological violence"—the rejection of Hinduism by people at the bottom of the caste hierarchy and the joining of its perceived enemy, Islam—proved more hurtful than physical violence. It shook the Hindu community. The conversions inspired a heated national debate in India and evoked militant reactions from the confessional patriots in the Hindu community, giving rise to the Hindu revivalism which has now become a major factor in Indian politics and society. Its popularity and dynamics even pushed the Congress-I, the ideologically centrist ruling party in the one-party system of India, into moving "dangerously close to becoming a Hindu confessional party."[3]

This book does not consider the conversions studied to be necessarily caused by a change of heart, which might have also occurred or may come gradually; it rather considers it a shrewd decision on the part of some aggressive untouchables to exit from the dominant Hindu community in protest and to accept Islam to increase their prospects of better life in Indian society. The study focuses equally on both aspects of the conversion process: leaving one religion and embracing another. Rejection of Hinduism and acceptance of Islam both satisfy the need for revenge and protest among untouchables, whereas the choice of Islam does have an element of social mobility because it brightens the chances of equal social status, as converts have perceived it. Considering the "this-worldliness" of these conversions, this analysis is about the sociological realities of the Hindu and Muslim communities rather than their religious belief systems.

The subject of study, however, remains untouchables—the actors; their state of progress in contemporary India; their current socioeconomic position; their level of untouchability today; their self-image; their aggressive behavior; how these conditions resulted in the decision of a few thousand untouchables to leave Hinduism; what they say they mean to achieve by this; and how this subjective component compares with the objective conditions in the society.

The main findings of this study are as follows. In recent years a substantial number of untouchables have achieved a relatively better economic and educational position. Perceiving themselves as equal in these respects to caste Hindus, they now aspire to the equal social status and treatment still being denied them by the caste-based society. Perception of this disjunction between expectation and reality is the main instigating factor of anti-Hindu feeling today. Different mediating factors have, however, led to different manifestations of aggressive behavior. A general increase in violence involving untouchables is one of the less sophisticated manifestations of their unorganized individual aggression. In the case of the conversions under study, the fact that conversion is a well-known option in South India, the ease of social contact with Tamil Muslims, the observation of Muslim egalitarianism, and the perception of Islam's opposition to Hinduism led them to the selection of Islam.

The Events Under Study

The 1981 religious conversion to Islam of untouchables in the South Indian state of Tamil Nadu forms the basis of this study. The number of converts was reported to range between two thousand and thirty-two thousand. The conversions resulted in the escalation of tension between religious communities: what Indians call communal tension. This tension reached the point of riots in many parts of the country. Untouchables and their problems had not attracted so much attention at the national level since Dr. Ambedkar, together with other untouchables, converted to Buddhism in 1956 [see Appendix II]. The Tamil Nadu conversions were preceded by caste Hindu/untouchable riots in 1978 in Maharashtra and anti-untouchable agitation in Gujarat in 1981. The Maharashtra riots were a backlash against demands to rename Marathwada University after the untouchable leader Dr. Ambedkar. In Gujarat, caste Hindus protested against reservations (quotas) for untouchables in medical colleges and more generally against the principle of reserving seats for underprivileged castes. By contrast, the Tamil Nadu conversions did not involve direct conflicts between caste Hindus and untouchables. Instead, conflict was mediated. This was possible because conversion to Islam involved symbolic rather than material and status issues and indirect expanding-sum rather than direct zero-sum status and material issues.

The latest official figures record a fourfold increase in atrocities against untouchables in the past few years.[4] The untouchables have not been passive in the face of this increasing violence. The Dalit Panthers in Maharashtra and the so-called Naxalites in Bihar and Tamil Nadu have helped to organize violent countermeasures.[5] This situation suggests that government programs of preferential treatment in education and services that benefit a large number of untouchables have not ended the troubles of this oppressed community.

The conversions and the increasing violence have raised many questions: Why are the untouchables resorting to extreme measures and conversion after a long period of protective discrimination and government welfare policies which benefit them? Are the recent conversions isolated cases or are they part of a larger phenomenon? Are there any socio-political determinants of conversion, or is it a fantasy solution to psychological stress, as some theories of religious conversion suggest? If, for example, conversion is a strategy of social mobility, why was Islam the religion chosen?

In search of answers to these questions, I have strayed into related issues without which explanation of the whole phenomenon might have been difficult. Changing attitudes among untouchables, the practice of untouchability in Indian society as a whole, and the particular situation in Tamil Nadu—especially of Tamil Muslims—are the topics I have discussed in detail. I have done so in order to provide the relevant background and perspective to understand the present phase of untouchables' aggressive behavior and the particular act of conversion.

Sources of Information

My sources include literature on political sociology and religious conversion, Indian government reports and documents for certain data on the scheduled castes (official term for untouchables in India), and newspaper and periodical coverage of current events. I have supplemented the documentary material with notes of interviews I conducted with twenty converts prior to the Meenakshipuram conversions. These interviews were held in the course of a short trip to South India, and were more the result of opportunity than science. I selected sixteen out of fifty students in a *madrasa* (a Muslim school), preferring the less vocal among them. Questions were not identical—I let their sense of relevance guide me. I met four other converts, and interviewed four leaders of Muslim organizations. One reporter of a national Indian daily newspaper helped me by providing unpublished texts of his detailed interviews with a few of the influential new Muslims.

Gathering information about the Muslim community, however, proved a comparatively more difficult task. No authentic data about the socio-economic position of Indian Muslims are available. The government census and sample survey organizations have the information, but they do not give out data by religion, on political grounds. This problem is reflected in the acute shortage of studies on the contemporary aspects of Indian Muslims' life. I have tried to overcome this problem by relying on secondary sources and non-official data.

Theoretical Perspective

Since my early observations suggested that the main variable in these conversions is the aggressive behavior among untouchables, I looked into the available theories in the literature of political sociology to explain the present aggressive phase of social change among the untouchables of India. The theoretical literature dealing with aggression, violence, and rebellion seemed more plausible in explaining the phenomenon under study. Almost all of the theories in this school have sprung from the psychological theory of frustration/aggression. This theory considers aggression a "natural" reaction to frustration.[6] This nexus has frequently been used to explain violent political behavior. The Feierabends are pioneers of research in political violence. They define their theory as follows:

> Frustration is the thwarting of or interference with the attainment of goals, aspirations, or expectations. On the basis of frustration aggression theory, it is postulated that frustration induced by the social system creates the social strain and discontent that in turn are the indispensable preconditions of violence.[7]

Although there is nothing wrong with this theory, it is a rather simple use of the frustration/aggression nexus. There is very little in the Feierabends' work that shows how this discontent or potential of violence leads to protest behavior. Tocqueville's concept of relative deprivation as defined by Gurr is a more useful and elaborate formulation of this thesis which will be discussed later.

Grimshaw, on the other hand, argues for the importance of social structure in interpreting collective violence:

> Superordinate/subordinate relationships in which parties are social categories are fundamentally unstable, and social violence is likely to occur when such an accommodative structure loses its viability.[8]

While Grimshaw's formulation seems to ignore unnecessarily the
weight of much history which suggests that the world has long lived
with stable asymmetry, it calls our attention to a social structural explanation. Turk's recent work gives more meaning to Grimshaw's
approach. Bringing in a perspective shaped by modern institutions and
modernization, he says, "The combination of deteriorating traditional
authority structures and conflict in the process of creating replace-
ments is likely to promote terrorism...."[9] This structural approach is
a macro-level explanation. By itself it is not useful in explaining why
some people in the same structural situation do react violently and
some do not. An answer to this question requires study of behavioral
factors, i.e., the individual and personality aspects of the actors.

Ted R. Gurr's *Why Men Rebel* is based mainly upon the concept of
relative deprivation. It provides a good explanatory framework for
analysis of the untouchables' current assertive and aggressive behavior. Alexis de Tocqueville originally brought this concept of relative
deprivation and rising expectation into currency by observing that the
strongholds of the French Revolution were exactly those areas in
which the greatest improvements in the standard of living had occurred.
The better-off French peasants revolted, not the bonded Germans.[10]
Relative deprivation describes a sense of disjunction between expectation and reality. Gurr defines it as

> ...actors' perception of discrepancy between their value expectations
> and their value capabilities. Value expectations are the goods and condi-
> tions of life to which people believe they are rightfully entitled. Value
> capabilities are the goods and conditions they think they are capable of
> getting and keeping.[11]

Gurr thinks that discontent arising from this perception of relative
deprivation is the basic instigating condition for participants in collective violence. His main emphasis is on perception of deprivation: on
how people feel it, not on objective reality:

> People may be subjectively deprived with reference to their expectations
> even though an objective observer might not judge them to be in want.
> Similarly, the existence of what the observer judges to be abject poverty
> or "absolute deprivation" is not necessarily thought to be unjust or
> irremediable by those who experience it.[12]

In distinguishing psychological from material deprivation, the concept of relative deprivation helps to explain, as Weiner says, "why
social protest, politicization, and increased participation often accom-
pany increasing income and improving living conditions—why rioters

in American urban ghettos are often not the poorest and not the un-employed...."[13]

Social conditions that increase the average level or intensity of expectations without increasing capabilities increase the intensity of discontent.[14] And this often happens in modernizing societies; as Huntington says, explaining his gap theory: "The ability of a transitional society to satisfy these new aspirations...increases much more slowly than the aspirations themselves."[15] Much of Gurr's work, however, talks about the preconditions of violence in detail. His significant contribution to the research on political violence is his discussion of mediating variables. He categorizes the determinants of the occurrence of aggressive behavior in two sets of variables: (1) instigating variables, (2) mediating variables. The social/psychological preconditions (i.e., deprivation-induced discontent) are the instigating variables which provide a "general spur" to an aggressive action. Mediating variables are the environmental and social conditions that determine the outcome of that energy by "inhibiting, facilitating, or rechanneling" its expressions:

> The more immediate psychological determinants of how we respond to specific deprivations are our cognitive maps of social causality and responsibility, by which we attribute blame, and our beliefs about the justifiability and consequences of specific kinds of actions in response to those situations.[16]

Gurr's works, like many other works in this discipline, are macro-level theories. They use aggregate economic, political, and social data at a national or cross-national level, which are more useful in determining what Gurr calls the "instigating" preconditions. They are less successful in explaining a particular act of aggressive action or the participation of people in specific forms of protest. For the same reasons the discussion of Davies and Hibbs' work, which could be applied only to widespread revolutionary activity, has been avoided.

My assumption is that as long as one relies only on aggregate data, the instigating conditions will remain more or less peripheral. The mediating variables need a more qualitative treatment of the situation and the actors. Therefore, the mediating variables of micro-level case studies will not benefit much from such macro-level works.[17]

Gurr also focuses on the conflict between rebels and regimes. He, like many others, does not define the theory at a level below that of the nation, i.e., between two social groups or communities. Thus methodologically it becomes impossible to create some of his complex indices, for example "the coercive balance" and "the balance of institutional support,'' in a study dealing with conflicts not involving regimes.

Although Gurr's mediating variables do take the actors' ''cognitive map'' into consideration, his argument remains rather deterministic. Nieburg's explanation, on the other hand, goes beyond the behavioral determinism of the psychological theories. It suggests that aggression can be purposive and designed to shape policy and behavior. Nieburg's definition of political violence, with special emphasis upon the concept of social bargaining, puts the intentions of the actors at the center:

> ...acts of disruption, destruction, injury whose purpose, choice of tar-
> gets or victims, surrounding circumstances, implementation, and/or
> effects have political significance, that is, tend to modify the behaviour
> of others in a bargaining situation that has consequences for the social
> system.[18]

Giving more importance to the actor's intention, however, Nieburg carefully states that ''. . . in many situations the escalation towards illegality and violence does not have to be inspired or planned. . . yet it becomes a part of the bargaining relationship.''[19] The phenomenon of conversion sounds more like a ''withdrawal'' from the bargaining process than participation in it. But, to borrow Hirschman's terminology, by this ''exit'' from the Hindu community—conversion—one does not stop being a member of the society in which the abhorrent caste system functions. One is still in the society, though outside that particular community. This exit/conversion, therefore, is ''a continuation of bargaining by other means,'' from without instead of within, and from a less disadvantageous position. Hirschman, though, says that exit from the traditional human groups is virtually unheard of. Our case study is one of its rare examples.[20]

What Hirschman is interested in is the ''recuperation mechanism'' of ''exit'' and ''voice.'' Conversion of untouchables is exit and voice both: exit from their caste and religious community and voice in the Indian society. Their action certainly has recuperative effects on the Hindu community the untouchables have left.

Conversion, however vocal an exit it may be, is not an act of violence, if violence is defined in strictly physical terms. Therefore, one can question the very use and relevance of the literature on violence in this study. There are many answers to this question: (1) Although the literature uses the term *violence*, what it is trying to explain is basically ''aggressive behavior.'' Physical violence is an extreme form of aggression. Protest can be another manifestation of aggression. It sometimes accompanies physical violence or results in it, or is marked by an occasional display of physical violence. (2) For semantic satisfaction one can use the term *psychological violence*, which occasionally appears in the literature. Gurr defines aggression as a "behavior designed to injure, physically or otherwise, those toward whom it is directed."[21] (3) The intentions of converts suggest that they did, as I will substantiate, mean to hurt the community they were to leave. One finds vengeful emotions in them. (4) Finally, although I am studying conversion as a case, it is only one of the manifestations of overall aggressive behavior among the untouchables of India, which involves physical violence as well.

2

Progress of the Untouchables and Society

Caste System in India

Caste—a given identity and a surname for almost everyone in India—confuses many who try to understand it from the outside. It is necessary, for the benefit of those not familiar with Indian society, to outline some of the main features of India's social order and the terms used in the contemporary studies of caste dynamics.

The word *caste* is not Indian originally. It was first used by non-Indians to clarify the social stratification in India, and its usage is itself part of the confusion. Now an established term in and out of India, it is used in lieu of the indigenuos Indian terms *varna* and *jati*. Some, however, prefer the word "caste" for *varna* and "sub-caste" for *jati*. The *varna*, literally "color" in Sanskrit, is the classic division of society in ancient Indo-Aryan life which later on acquired a place in the Hindu scriptures. There are four varnas, which are ranked hierarchically. The first three varnas are the Brahmins ("priests"); the Kshatriyas ("rulers" and "warriors"); and the Vaisyas ("merchants"). These traditionally literate first three varnas are also called twice-born ("spiritually initiated"). The fourth and lowest varna is that of the Shudras ("common people," who were barred from knowledge of the sacred texts). Dasas ("scavengers" and "sweepers") were untouchables, outside this varna system; thus the term *avarna* ("outcaste"). Sociologists suggest that this varna system was more a traditional "social ideology" than a strict social reality.

In India today, Brahmins at the top of varna hierarchy and untouchables outside but still at the bottom of it are more easily recognizable identities than the other three varnas. Politically, anti-Brahmin movements in Tamil Nadu and untouchable mobilization all over India reflect their differentiated position in Indian society. It is estimated that the first three varnas comprise 17.58 percent of the Indian population.[22] But, because of their traditional advantage, they are disproportionately represented in the Indian socio-political elite. They played a leading role in the independence movement. They are considered to be the "forward classes" of Indian society, in comparison to the "backward classes"—another term in the caste jargon of the sociopolitical competition of India. They loosely consist of the *shudra varna*, or jatis that lie in between the higher three castes and the untouchables. They number about 44 percent.[23] As the above discussion suggests, varna categories do have some contemporary relevance. They loosely correspond to certain sets of socio-economic demands in India.

But it is the term *jati* which is commonly used in India, far more often than *varna*. Jati is the social reality of everyday life. It has been estimated that there are three thousand jatis in India. Everyone knows what his jati is, although possibly some may not be sure about their jati's placement in the varna system. There are numerous jatis in each varna. However, it is not always easy to categorize clearly each jati in a varna, especially between Kshatriyas and Shudras. It is also not uncommon to see clusters of different jatis with a common name and a level of shared characteristics. Some jatis, because of their numerical strength concentrated in a particular locality, become powerful enough to interpret and enforce *dharma* (the Hindu sacred code of life) in their areas despite the fact that some members of a higher varna are living in those localities. These locally "dominant castes" play an important role in the social, political, and economic life of that area: for example in a given electoral constituency, or in a particular caste conflict.

A jati is an endogenous group whose membership is hereditarily determined. Each jati is hierarchically ranked according to the ritual purity of its traditional occupation, even if that occupation is not pursued in fact. Members of jatis can be distinguished by their mannerisms, life style, and dress. The relationship of a lower jati to a higher jati is governed by *dharma*, the sacred and traditional prescription of Hindu life describing the rules and prohibitions of inter-dining and inter-marriage and so on. Deviation from dharma may be punished by the *jati panchayat* ("elders' council") or it may invite the wrath of a higher varna or a dominant jati against the defiant individual or his jati as a whole.

Untouchables at the Bottom of Caste Hierarchy

According to the 1981 census, fifteen percent of the Indian population belong to jatis considered untouchables (105 million).[24] Untouchability was abolished by the Indian constitution, but not the caste system in general. This social system, sanctioned by Hindu socio-religious tradition, has its most powerful hold in rural India, where 80 percent of the population lives.

Untouchables traditionally compose the most well-defined and the most socially differentiated set of jatis. Historically, they knew themselves by the names of their particular jatis and occupations, although they suffered from the common untouchable status assigned to them by Hindu scriptures and society. The British official term for untouchables, "scheduled castes," is still used in India, but the first common name adopted by some untouchables themselves, as they acquired consciousness of their common sufferings, is *Adi Dravida* (meaning "original members of the Dravidian race"). The Adi Dravida movement (since 1918) in Madras was also the first to formulate the concept that untouchable jatis were the original inhabitants of India.[25] Later, when Gandhi took up the cause of untouchables, he christianized them as *Harijans* ("children of God"). *Harijan* is now the usual term for untouchables in India. Militant untouchables and some other radicals, however, prefer the term *Dalits* ("oppressed people").[26]

The fair-skinned Aryans who came to India in 1500 BC started calling the conquered indigenous people *dasas* (literally "slaves"). They were of dark complexion and were regarded as inferior to Aryans. These dasas were excluded from the social life of Aryans and were eventually relegated to the menial jobs. This social status was later legitimized by the religious sanctions of pollution and purity. Hindu religious books, on the other hand, regard untouchables to be the

offspring of mixed marriages and illicit unions. The first account of untouchability as a social reality is available through the observations of
Alberuni (AD 1020), a Muslim scientist visiting India. He noted two occupational endogenous groups named Dom and Chandala that lived outside villages and had limited interaction with others. Untouchables in
Indian villages today still live in hamlets outside the main village. Later
British colonial officer/sociologists provide us with plenty of information
on how they found untouchability practiced in India. J.H. Hutton's work
is regularly referred to in this regard.[27] The following list, compiled by
Marc Galanter, gives a broad idea of what untouchability means for these
jatis and their members at the bottom of the social hierarchy where there
are many disabilities but hardly any privileges.

> Denial or restriction of access to public facilities, such as wells, schools,
> roads, post offices, and courts.
>   Denial or restriction of access to temples where their presence might
> pollute the deity as well as the higher caste worshippers, and from rest-
> houses, tanks, and shrines connected to temples. Untouchables. . . are
> forbidden to learn the vedas (the earliest and most sacred books of
> orthodox Hinduism).
>   Exclusion from any honorable, and most profitable, employment
> and relegation to dirty or menial occupations.
>   Residential segregation. . . by requiring them to remain outside the
> village.
>   Denial of access to services such as those provided by barbers, laun-
> drymen, restaurants, shops, and theaters or requiring the use of sepa-
> rate utensils and facilities within such places.
>   Restrictions on style of life, especially in the use of goods indicating
> comfort or luxury. Riding on horseback, use of bicycles, umbrellas,
> footwear, the wearing of gold and silver ornaments, the use of palan-
> quins to carry bridegrooms. . .
>   Requirements of deference in forms of address, language, sitting and
> standing in presence of higher castes.
>   Restrictions on movement. Untouchables might not be allowed on
> roads and streets within prescribed distance of the houses or persons of
> higher castes.
>   Liability to unremunerated labor for the higher castes and to the
> performance of menial services for them.[28]

Socio-Economic Conditions
of Untouchables Today

As far as the economic condition of today's untouchables is concerned, it is not as miserable as it appears in the early sociological

accounts of the British period when Christian missionaries started their welfare programs for untouchables. The pathetic socio-economic situation of untouchables became a point of sympathetic attention and welfare policy in the British period. Then the cause of the untouchables was taken up by the nationalist movement. Opposition to untouchability became an integral part of the national agenda. The constitution of 1951 provided proportional representation for untouchables in the parliament and legislatures, and reservation in educational institutions and in civil services. It also asked for special economic benefits.[29] These constitutional protections and their implementation have helped untouchables improve their lot significantly. I will try to suggest the degree and level of this change and the proportions of untouchables affected.

For most people, government service is still the most attractive career in India. Government service provides incentives for higher education, and has prestige as well as security and relatively good pay. The following numbers show a considerable improvement for untouchables in this category.

Table 1

Officer-Level Representation of Untouchables in All-India Services as the percentage of the total number of officers

Name of Service	As of 1/1/54	As of 1/1/79
Indian Administrative Service	1.63%	9.69%
Indian Police Service	1.19%	9.22%
Indian Foreign Service	N.A. (As of 1/1/59, 1.67%)	12.32%

Sources: India, Office of the Commissioner for Scheduled Castes and Scheduled Tribes: *Report of the Commissioner for Scheduled Castes and Scheduled Tribes 1955* (5th Report), p. 111; *1960-61* (10th Report), p.288; *1978-79* (26th Report), Appendix, p. 28 [hereafter cited as *Commissioner*].

Note: Selection of services here reported was limited to the available comparative data for the early period.

These figures show that at officer-level positions in these prestigious services, the share of untouchables has yet to grow to their 14.6 percent proportion of the total population. Nevertheless, it is a significant improvement over the past. Untouchables account for 15.12 percent of all central government employees. This better picture is due to their oversubscription at the Class IV level of employment (excluding sweepers, a traditional occupation for untouchables). The impact of the policies of progressive discrimination for untouchables could be better understood if we contrast it with the Muslim minority, which is not enjoying any preference of this kind (see Table 1a).

Table 1a

Untouchables and Muslims Representation in
Central Government Services of India Compared

As Percentage of Total Employees

	Untouchables (as of 1/1/1979)	Muslims (as of 1/1/1980)
Class I	4.75%	1.61%
Class II	7.37%	3.00%
Class III	12.55%	4.41%
Class IV (excluding sweepers)	19.32%	5.12%

Sources: Commissioner 1979, p. 25; Paper circulated by Minorities Commission, New Delhi, as quoted by *Muslim India* 1 (Dec. 1983): 552.

Note: Muslims are 11.21 percent of the total Indian population, whereas untouchables are 14.6 percent of the same, according to the 1971 census.

According to one conservative estimate, more than a million untouchables are employed in the public and semi-public sectors.[30] Though a majority of them may not belong to the middle class, they have job security and are not economically dependent on the traditional sources of income. Another million untouchables are looking for the same kinds of jobs.[31] Over eight million untouchables are independent cultivators.[32] However small their income may be, they are not dependent as agricultural laborers are, subject to many forms of exploitation. A substantial number of untouchables other than these are self-employed or in the private sector. Around ten million out of eighty million untouchables are literate, and more than 75.5 percent of untouchable children in the relevant age group go to school.[33]

The above-mentioned people, one million public servants and one million job seekers and eight million cultivators, add up to a considerable number. The total equals the untouchables' literacy figure of 1971, i.e., ten million.[34] However, all these literates may not necessarily be economically independent, or a majority of those economically independent may not be literate. One should keep in mind, however, that even if these people are not more than ten million, they all have families who share their improved fortunes. If they are enjoying a life different from their ancestors'—relatively economically independent, and literate—their independence, aspirations, and experience must be a part of their families' social mobility. Considering the average family size in India, 5.6, this circle expands to fifty-six million untouchables—more than half of the total untouchable population.

Furthermore, there may be a greater concentration of untouchable families commanding these advantages in one village than another. If government jobs, land, and literacy mean independence and prestige, individuals, families and villages who command these are more powerful than others. Mencher has studied continuity and change among untouchables in a few Tamil Nadu villages where the literacy level among untouchables was almost the same as in the general population. Noting the superior position of the untouchables in one village, and the more relaxed state of untouchables and caste-Hindu relations there, she says, "It appears to be due in part to the presence of several well-to-do and able Paraiyans [an untouchable caste]..." or as one untouchable person said, "In our village, we are in a majority and some of us have property, so we can be bold."[35]

Untouchability in Society

I have tried to suggest some of the changes in occupation and education of untouchables that have flowed from legally mandated progressive discrimination. What changes have occurred in the values of society and in the practice of untouchability? A discussion about the availability of water to untouchables will help explain the situation. Water, an essential for life, has been a problem for untouchables. The basis of discrimination in allowing the use of water sources to all sections of the community is the Hindu belief that water sources are polluted if they are touched by untouchables. The commissioner for scheduled castes and scheduled tribes in his _Report for 1977-78_ has discussed at length the discrimination practiced against untouchables in the use of drinking water sources in rural areas:

The approximate percentage of villages in the four groups may be as follows:

I. Villages where scheduled castes [untouchables] and caste Hindus have common sources of drinking water without any discrimination: 5 percent

II. Villages where scheduled castes are allowed to use common sources of drinking water with some restrictions which indicates the prevalence of untouchability: 10 percent

III. Villages where scheduled castes have their own sources of drinking water and indicates the prevalence of untouchability: 75 percent

IV. Villages where scheduled castes are not allowed to use common sources of drinking water. The drinking water is generally poured in their pots by caste Hindus or the scheduled castes have to go to fetch water from agricultural wells or springs and rivers: 10 percent[36]

Thus, untouchability is prevalent in about 95 percent of villages regarding access to the water sources.

This situation of untouchability also differs from region to region and most probably from village to village. A survey conducted by the All India Harijan Sevak Sangh makes this clear. In Madurai District of Tamil Nadu, the Sangh found 100 percent of the public wells in the surveyed villages not accessible to the untouchables.[37] These data show that a positive change in the condition of untouchables still coincides with the continued practice of untouchability.

The Behavioral Disrespect for Untouchables

Although aggregate data as given above provide essential information, they do not come close to conveying how it feels to be an untouchable. Many of the practices of untouchability are merely deliberate or nonarticulated behavioral displays of disrespect for untouchables. An analysis of the official *Meenakshipuram Report*, as published in *Sunday*, November 7-13, 1982, will give a glimpse of this problem. This federal government study deals with the problems and conflicts leading to untouchables' conversions in Meenakshipuram.

The report renders evidence of how subtly attitudes towards untouchability can be conveyed. It mentions many names from Thevar caste Hindu, untouchable, and Muslim communities. Its usage of the Indian title *Shri* (a sign of respect), whether intentional or unconscious, provides an interesting insight. All seven members of the Hindu delegation to the investigators are honored with the title. All four members of the Muslim delegation are distinguished by *Shri* and *Sahib* both, which is like putting "Mr." before and "Esq." after an English name. But none of the five members of the untouchable delegation is accorded any title whatsoever. In the discussion of a criminal case filed in court, all three accused Thevar caste Hindus—two of whom were convicted—are called *Shri*, two accused new-Muslims are called *Shri*, but among the fourteen accused untouchables—none convicted, and one of whom happened to be an attorney himself—none is given the honorific. An official response might be that this is just a mistake by a careless typist. But that reflects how attitudes and behavior towards untouchables persist. This "overlooking" becomes serious because of the fact that this study is done by the federal investigators in collaboration with the local administration, and the subject under investigation is nothing less than the question of justice, honor, equality, and self-respect for untouchables.

Continued untouchability along with the improved economic situation is giving rise to the occurences of untouchability offenses and atrocities against untouchables. A study of the cases registered from 1955 to 1978 under the Untouchability Offenses Act (now Protection of Civil Rights Act—PCR hereafter), shows that there has been a multiple increase in the seventies (unlike the sixties, which showed a small decrease from the fifties—see Table 2). This growth may be due to rising consciousness among untouchables which leads them to report more offenses, or it can be a result of increased offenses as untouchables begin to challenge the social order, or both.

Table 2

Increase or Decrease in the Numbers of Cases
Registered Under the Untouchability Offenses Act
(Later Protection of Civil Right Act), 1955-78

Period	Avg. Cases per Year	Ten Year Average	Percentage of Change
1955-1959	479.20		
1960-1964	453.60 ⎫		
1965-1969	350.00 ⎭	401.80	−16.15%
1970-1974	1,453.00 ⎫		
1975-1978	4,079.30 ⎭	2,766.15	+588.44%

Sources: Calculations are based upon the data in *Report of the Commissioner, 1971-72* and *1972-73,* p. 343; *1975-76* and *1976-77,* I:103; *1977-78,* 1:118; *1978-79,* II:137.

Note: I have not used per-year data, because fluctuations are mainly due to the incompleteness of the figures from different states. Period analysis not only balances out this difference but gives an understanding of the trend.

Not only do practices persist about which untouchables increasingly complain, there seems also to be an increasing number of atrocities against untouchables. Murder, rape, arson, and other violent acts against untouchables are registered against offenders under the Indian Penal Code. There was a 75.55 percent increase in 1977 and about 143 percent in 1978 in the numbers of reported atrocities from the base figures of 1976.[38] The occurrence of atrocities, however, varies from region to region, as shown in Table 3.

Table 3

Contrast between the Number of Cases of
Untouchability Offenses and Atrocities

State	Cases of Untouchability (PCR) in 1978 per million scheduled castes*	Cases of Atrocities in 1978 per million scheduled castes
Tamil Nadu	74.82	17.78
Gujarat	393.40	296.70
Maharashtra	424.83	346.35
UP	15.48	305.28
Bihar	6.41	240.30

Source: Calculations based upon data in *Commissioner, 1978-79,* 1:187, 231.
Note: The data on atrocities have been available since 1974, but the comparable state-wide data of the cases registered under PCR are not available for 1974, '75, and '76. The data for 1977 are also incomplete. Therefore, it is difficult to study the trend. However, the incomplete data have the same features shown in this table.
*official term for untouchables.

These figures represent an almost classic case of the problems posed by raw social statistics. Greater atrocities in Uttar Pradesh (UP) and Bihar than in Tamil Nadu may be related to a generally higher rate of reported violence in those states. They may show that the low number of PCR cases in UP and Bihar is due to a lack of initiative on the part of untouchables, and to a higher level of coercion. So far as the variation in untouchability offenses is concerned, higher rates may be a good rather than a bad sign, showing greater willingness by untouchables to report offenses, while low rates may reflect greater coercion by upper castes. Reports of atrocities are not necessarily the result of actions by the victims, while registering a PCR case to a certain extent requires the victim's initiative. This suggests an important difference in the consciousness of untouchables in different regions.

Modernization appears to be an important variable. Maharashtra and Tamil Nadu have the highest literacy rate for untouchables in India. Maharashtra, Tamil Nadu, and Gujarat also have the highest urbanization rates in India (32.03 percent, 32.98 percent and 31.08 percent respectively, as compared to an all-India rate of 23.73 percent) while Bihar and UP have the lowest proportions of literates and urban residents.[39] Whatever the causes, this variation does point out the regional differences and variations in the situation and in the problems of untouchables. Such variations in the level of modernization and untouchability sometimes exist among villages in the same region as well.

Tamil Nadu Society and Untouchability

According to the census of 1971, the population of Tamil Nadu is 41.1 million. About 71 percent of these are caste Hindus, 18 percent untouchables, 6 percent Christians, and 5 percent Muslims. In India, Tamil Nadu stands seventh in population, but in literacy (39.46 percent in 1971) and in numbers of registered medical practitioners, Tamil Nadu stands second in the country.[40] About 64 percent of the untouchable workers in Tamil Nadu are agricultural laborers, whereas only 30.46 percent of the total Tamil Nadu workers are agricultural laborers. Of the untouchable work force in Tamil Nadu, about 18 percent are cultivators as compared to about 31 percent of the total workers in Tamil Nadu who are cultivators.[41]

South India, having been only lightly touched by the influence of Islam during the period of Mughal rule in the north, represents today a bastion of traditional Hinduism. South Indian Hindus adhere very scrupulously to the ancient rules concerning purity and pollution. Tamil Nadu (or old Madras State) in the extreme south of India historically has a negative image among the Indian states in regard to the strict observance of caste and untouchability. Hutton's early description of Tamil untouchability is still being quoted by sociologists. The national press featured this negative image as a cause of conversion.[42] This popular stereotype has overshadowed the fact that Madras (later Tamil Nadu) was the first state to rebel against the caste system and to initiate reforms of its hierarchical and discriminatory practices.

The breast-cloth controversy of the early nineteenth century and the early opening of temples in the princely state now included in Tamil Nadu called Travencore (1936) and then in Madras (1939) were the first in India and are among the examples of early reform in what is now Tamil Nadu. The untouchables' struggle to wear breast cloths typifies their situation in the nineteenth century. It also indicates the forces of change working at that time. The controversy occurred in southern Travencore where, as in many other parts of nineteenth-century India, dress symbolized hierarchical status and the subjection and domination that accompanied them. The Nadars (an untouchable caste), like other untouchable castes, were categorically forbidden to cover their breasts at any time. In the early nineteenth century, Nadar converts to Christianity as well as non-Christian enlightened Nadar women started covering their breasts. This assertion of equality on the part of untouchables, perhaps merely an attempt to practice the newly acquired standard of decency, was considered an act of defiance by the higher castes. It resulted in clashes and riots between the untouchable Nadars and the higher castes. By 1859, the governor of Madras had to interfere by granting permission to Nadar women to wear a cloth over their breasts and shoulders, with the restriction that apparel above the waist should not resemble the dress used by women of high castes.[43]

Tamil Nadu was among the first areas to receive Christian missionaries, their schools and hospitals. Religious conversion for the sake of social mobility was used as early as the eighteenth century by southern untouchables. Untouchables of this region were also first in making some attempts in the nineteenth century at improving their social status through "sanskritization."[44] By the early twentieth century, they had turned to the British administration to raise their status and to express their grievances against the dominant groups. The Self Respect movement, the anti-Brahmin movement, and the Dravida Kazhagam party all in one way or another addressed the same social questions. Later the Tamil separatist party Dravida Munnetra Kazhagam (DMK, formed in 1949) inherited some of Naicker's ideology.[45]

The DMK and its splinter ADMK parties have been criticized by their untouchable supporters for negligence in the implementation of the party's radical social reform ideology. They are accused of failure to revive the pre-Aryan ideal of a "Tamil casteless society."[46] Nevertheless, a relatively closer attention by DMK and ADMK governments to the untouchables' cause and welfare is reflected in the available data. The expenditure incurred during the years 1974-77 on the untouchables'

Table 5

Proportion of Untouchables in All-India and Tamil Nadu Services
Compared: Untouchables as Percentage of Total Employees

Name of Service	Class I	Class II	Class III
All India services as of 1/1/75	3.43%	4.98%	10.71%
Tamil Nadu services as of 3/31/75	4.00%	10.86%	11.00%

Sources: Commissioner, 1977-79, 2:25, and 1977-78, 2:23.
Note: This includes information from 96 departments out of 123 and includes data of scheduled tribes. Since there is no separate reservation for scheduled castes and scheduled tribes in Tamil Nadu, no breakdown is available (commissioner's note). However, scheduled tribes account for a small difference.

State of Legal Protection for Untouchables

As mentioned before, Tamil Nadu is not among the worst states of India as far as the reported atrocities are concerned. In 1978, there were only 17.78 per million violent crimes against untouchables. However, the reported instances of untouchability offenses (which require some action by the victims) under the PCR Act are four times higher than the figures of atrocities (see Table 3). Due to the better modernization level, untouchables in Tamil Nadu are much more likely to register complaints than in UP or Bihar, where the actual practice of untouchability is believed to be higher than in Tamil Nadu.

The Tamil Nadu government has set up mobile police squads in six districts. They visit interior villages for proper and speedy investigation of all complaints under the Protection of Civil Rights Act. A general look through the available figures of the justice system suggests that Tamil Nadu's system of justice is the best among the Indian states. Of the 590 PCR cases in 1978, only 17.96 percent remained pending in courts. This figure is the lowest among Indian states, where 98.46 percent of cases in Bihar, 60.96 percent of cases in Gujarat, 83.27 percent of cases in Maharashtra, and 94.13 percent of cases in UP remained pending. Even in terms of time elapsed in disposing of cases, none of the cases pending in Tamil Nadu were with police and courts for more than six months. This is again the highest level of efficiency as compared to the above-mentioned states. Of all Indian cases which ended in conviction in 1978, 42.71 percent were carried out by the Tamil Nadu judiciary.[52] However, this judicial performance does not mean a rule of law in Tamil Nadu. This progress report deals only with the registered cases. The Tamil Nadu police are increasingly earning a bad name for taking sides with the dominant castes and for the harsh treatment of untouchable activists. Many cases of untouchability and atrocities are dismissed even before they are officially registered, due to the partisan attitude of police. Maltreatment of untouchables is one of the major complaints.[53] The press has consistently mentioned a police/caste axis and extra-legal police violence in the reports following the 1980-1981 conversions.

The high level of judicial efficiency in registered cases for the protection of untouchables in Tamil Nadu has a limited impact on the society because the occurrence of cases is merely seventy-five per million untouchables. Such a low ratio of cases brought to court hardly touches the behavior deeply entrenched in the values of the population at large. This certainly does not pose any challenge to the practice of untouchability, widespread in rural Tamil Nadu. According to a survey, in 77.7 percent of the 148 villages surveyed in three districts of Tamil Nadu, public wells are not accessible to untouchables, and in about 92 percent of the villages temples are not open to them. This survey also reports that untouchability is widely practiced in restaurants, barbershops, and laundries.[54] The deputy commissioner for scheduled castes has noted that untouchability in respect to water is more pronounced in six districts of Tamil Nadu compared to ninety-two other Indian districts.[55]

3

The Nature of Violence
and Little Ambedkars

The term *atrocities* against untouchables is normally used in the Indian press and the relevant literature to describe violent events involving untouchables. But this use needs clarification. It connotes passivity on the part of the untouchables, which I think is not always the case. The term has not been defined by the penal laws, but the Commission for Scheduled Castes lists murder, rape, arson, and violence (which are taken note of under the Indian Penal Code) as atrocities if they are committed against untouchables. Whereas cases of violence involving untouchables are often multi-dimensional, the available breakdown of statistics is available only by crime. A detailed study of court decisions to classify the nature and motivation of these atrocities would help to determine their real nature accurately (cf. Table 3).

The office of the commissioner, however, has categorized the complaints it received directly from untouchables. According to these categories, 54.71 percent of the 1,473 complaints received in 1977-78 concerned land, agriculture, housing, education, and so forth, while 45.29 percent were cases of harassment and untouchability. In 1978-79, the breakdown of 1,890 complaints was 58.88 percent and 41.11 percent in these respective categories.[56] Although it is a loose measure, one can assume on the basis of the commissioner's classification that less than half of the untouchables' complaints are related to classical untouchability

and more than half are the result of economic grievances among untouchables. Even in the broader category, the complaints themselves
must be the acts of very aware and informed untouchables, because the
commissioner's office is not as known and accessible as the police station.
The increased government figures for cases of atrocities and untouchability (see Tables 2 and 3) have been considered a sign of increasing literacy
and confidence among untouchables.[57] Reporting these things to the
authorities is in itself a challenge to the traditional system, i.e., an act
of defiance against the classical rights of the dominant castes. If one
did not resist wrongs or demand rights,there would be no problem.

Patterns of Violence

A single act of reporting atrocities to the police, objecting to untouchability, or a demand for proper wages by one individual untouchable
in a village is capable of creating a breach in the power relations of that
village by challenging the classical pattern in which untouchables are
expected to be passive. This rebellious behavior often gives rise to fear
and anger in the dominant caste. The dominant caste, considering the
challenge a mark of the changing times, may swallow it, or may engage
in a planned or unplanned punishment. The whole dominant caste
community may be involved in punishing untouchables as some members of the dominant caste may take it upon themselves to teach them
a lesson. Sometimes, the result is direct physical attack. For example,
in the massacres of Deoli (Uttar Pradesh) and Kestara (Madhya Pradesh) in 1981 and 1982, untouchables were punished because of their
having approached the judicial system.[58] Sometimes this punishment
is indirect, through some anonymous robbers, as was the case in the
unresolved massacre of Sadhupur (UP).[59] It is a common practice to
fabricate stories to register with police against untouchables by mani-
pulating the local police and administrative apparatus to teach a lesson
to the untouchables. At occasions teasing and minor individual clashes
lead both communities to confront each other. Individual cases of atrocity are also likely to become a symbolic issue if local untouchables have
political activists among them. Symbolic issues are likely to arise, however, where locally accumulated outrage against the day-to-day practice
of untouchability already exists.

Today, increasingly, untouchables defend against these attacks
and sometimes try to preempt them. As a result both communities

suffer damage, though untouchables normally suffer more than others. This could be called a communal riot. It may be a spontaneous outburst followed by escalating hostile relationships, such as the Villumpuram riot in Tamil Nadu.[60]

Another form of conflict is the planned mobilization of a dominant caste group for their economic interest, such as that of the Thakurs' (a landowning caste) solidarity against the untouchables of Bihar or the Maharashtra caste students' mobilization against neo-Buddhists (untouchable converts to Buddhism), or the anti-reservation movement in Gujarat (against quotas for untouchables). Sometimes untouchables also resort to planned mobilization of the oppressed untouchables for a violent strategy of change, such as the so-called Naxalite movement in Bihar and Tamil Nadu, or the Dalit Panther movement in Maharashtra.

This assertiveness of untouchable individuals and communities is the main cause of the dominant castes' outraged attitude. The challenge to the traditional authority was the main reason for the Deoli (UP) and Kestara (MP) massacres. In both, untouchable individuals had pursued their cases in the courts against the untouchability offenses of the high caste Thakurs and Yadavas. All the instances of collective atrocities investigated by the commissioner in 1977-78 and 1979 have one thing in common: assertiveness and the resistance of untouchable individuals and communities against wrongs done them.

The form, shape and implicit or explicit nature of all the above-mentioned categories vary from village to village and region to region, according to the socio-economic situation of untouchables and their power relationship with the dominant caste in a given area.

Who Are These Assertive People?

Are all untouchables socio-economically alike? Certainly not. In the cases of the Deoli and Kestara massacres, newspaper reports make it evident that in both the villages untouchables were economically better off than the general lot. Their spotlessly clean neighborhoods had brick houses. Due to their economic position, untouchables in both villages had a background of assertiveness and disobedience to Yadavas. In Deoli the untouchables' leader had been killed in an earlier dispute, and in Kestara the victims belonged to a prosperous and assertive untouchable extended family. Clearly, in both the cases, their assertiveness was a result of economic independence. They were conscious of their rights and had information about government agencies from which to seek help.[61]

In the Maharashtra riots of 1978, the commissioner himself noted a common pattern in Kanderi Village. Only the houses of those who owned land and businesses were burnt. In other villages as well, the commissioner has noted that assertive individuals and untouchable school teachers were specially targeted and hunted down.[62] The Belchi massacre (Bihar) in 1977 became famous because of the political attention it garnered. The ingredients for upheaval in that situation included the facts that the village had electricity, an untouchable teacher was giving special attention to the untouchable children, and a politically conscious untouchable young man was organizing the youths for better wages.[63] In Gujarat, studies indicate that "support for the pro-reservation movement tended to come from the most economically advanced [untouchable] castes."[64]

These instances suggest that those untouchables who have benefitted from the modernization process, and are literate and economically independent, are more assertive. This is at least the picture that emerges from examining the many cases of atrocities that have occurred since 1981. The conclusion is supported by several public opinion surveys, which show that a higher socio-economic status correlates with potential radicalization. In a survey of untouchable government employees, in response to the question, "should untouchables wait until caste Hindus give up the practice of untouchability or should they act on their own," 50 percent of the uneducated untouchables as against 25.8 percent of untouchable graduates recommended a soft line; their response varied between resignation and the hope of being able to convince caste Hindus. In contrast, 74.2 percent of the highly educated untouchables pleaded for stronger reactions; 57.1 percent of them even supported the use of violence.[65]

In some instances, uneducated agricultural laborers have also tried to organize and demand their rights, but most were organized and motivated by some political activists. A few educated untouchable *baboos* ("low-paid white-collar workers") and some untouchable landowners in a village with enough untouchables to hold the balance of numerical power can assure untouchables of that village to assert themselves, hoping to resist the backlash and to force the other party to adopt an attitude of indifference.

The degree of perception of the suffering caused by untouchability also increases with a rising educational standard. This perception does not necessarily correlate with any personal experience of untouchability. In the above-mentioned survey of government employees who have materially benefitted from the preferential policies, 75.7 percent of the graduate untouchables are of the opinion that untouchability is still practiced in most parts of India, whereas only 22.6 percent of the illiterate untouchable employees think so.[66] Assuming that untouchables with low socio-economic status suffer under untouchability to a larger extent than those with high status, these responses seem to be more a result of the extent of awareness than the function of actual personal experience. Keeping in mind this correlation of better socio-economic status to greater perception of suffering and greater readiness to fight back, Tamil Nadu untouchables' relatively greater aggressiveness is understandable.

More Aggressive Untouchables of Tamil Nadu

It is possible that Tamil Nadu untouchables have shown more aggressiveness than those in other states in India. This observation is based upon a few studies relating to particular villages, but the generalization has the problem that villages vary in the socio-economic level of their untouchable communities. Mencher has worked in two hamlets of untouchables. She has pointed out the change in untouchables' attitudes in one of her two villages with a better status and characterized it as rebellious. She found that extramarital affairs across caste and out caste lines were tolerated as long as violence did not erupt. The majority of instances noted in this village involved untouchable men with Naicker (a non-untouchable caste) women. Although there are proverbs in various Indian languages which take a light view of sexual molestation of untouchable women, affairs between untouchable men and higher caste women are intolerable in the eyes of *Manu* (Hindu sacred law) and society and normally invite harsh punishment from the higher caste. Thus, the tolerance of such a situation in Mencher's village is significant. On the other hand, in a nearby village with less economic independence, untouchables did not enjoy this "liberty of defiance."[67]

In the 1978 Tamil Nadu riots, caste Hindus attacked the untouchables' area first, killing twelve people, but the untouchables' retaliation resulted in caste Hindus suffering more. Houses of 63 untouchables—as compared to 115 houses and 15 shops of non-untouchables—were damaged. A total of 112 untouchable and 174 nonuntouchable families were affected by these riots.[68]

Let us look into a case of even higher aggression. In early 1981, Ramanathapuram District (Tamil Nadu) experienced a series of caste troubles. A research team found that in Prachur and Wail villages an "aggression" of untouchables turned into riots. In the first village, untouchables had their own shops and a milk sellers' association. Their students attended a nearby college. They were agitating against verbal insults and untouchability offenses. In the second village, 250 of 750 families were untouchables. Here also they attacked the high caste with outside untouchable help and gave them "a lesson," in return for the times high caste persons had beaten untouchables when they were alone and the police were not there to help them.[69]

The Kanyakumari and Gulandi (Tamil Nadu) caste clashes of 1982 were also the result of conscious and organized Christian untouchables defending their rights and responding to caste offenses.[70]

These cases suggest that (1) "atrocity" is an inadequate term for violence involving untouchables, since they do not always take a passive role as the word connotes. (2) Instead, "clash," "riot," or "conflict" should be the vocabulary to define present violence between untouchables and caste-Hindu communities. (3) Sometimes untouchables, for the sake of justice, resort to violence first or provoke it with the conscious objectives of deterrence, retaliation, and preemption. (4) Untouchables are increasingly depending upon themselves for protection. (5) Incidents of violence are scattered around the country. There is no organizational or communication link among these groups. They neither belong to a particular caste nor are they members of a particular party or followers of any single leader. In most of the cases it was at the initiative of someone in the village, not by outside inspiration, that untouchables took a stand and asserted themselves. The exception is the Naxalite mobilization in Bihar, although it should be noted that many recent episodes of "Naxalism" are merely isolated cases of untouchable assertiveness which are branded Naxalism for easier prosecution of militants.

Little Ambedkars

There is a stratum of untouchable individuals which is the product of political and economic modernization, as discussed in the preceding chapter. These people are informed about their rights and are conscious of the plight of their community. They are beyond the era of hero-following. Gandhi, Ambedkar, and Jagjivan Ram are matters of the past for them. They think on their own feet about themselves and their community. In a given situation, they assert themselves and provide leadership to a family, hamlet, or village. As independent individuals, they say what they feel and do what they like. In this way their actions are different from earlier sorts of caste assertions—from the Nadar association in Tamil Nadu, or from the type of movement embodied by the Mahar untouchable caste in Maharashtra, who converted in large numbers to Buddhism under the leadership of Dr. Ambedkar. These movements were collective, caste-based, concentrated in a certain region, and led by charismatic caste leadership.[71] This new stratum is also not a part of any Naxalite type of organization, with some exceptions.

I would call these individual souls "little Ambedkars," after the famous untouchable leader. They are masters of their own fates. They are more sensitive than other untouchables. They feel more sharply and assert what they feel. Consequently, the atrocities against untouchables and the occurrence of massacres increase in number. Because of their constant resistance or response to violence, these "little Ambedkars" are sometimes bracketed with Naxalites. If they are successful in limiting the excesses of caste people, by forcing them to adopt an attitude of tolerance toward their community, their efforts go unnoticed by the media. It is their failures, resulting in violent clashes, on the other hand, which find a place in the newspapers.

4

Untouchables' Conflict With the Dominant Castes

The values of modernization are different in some very important ways from those of Hindu tradition. If the central values of Hindu tradition are hierarchy, continuity, and transcendence; those of modernization are equality, individualism, and rationalism. Many untouchables have undergone this process of "value conversion." Equality of status is their main goal. And this is the only criterion by which they judge people. They are simply not prepared to accept the status traditionally ascribed to them. They are young and militant. Unlike their forebears, they have become acutely aware of their ritual and socio-economic subjugation and are impatient to get out of it. They are aware of their constitutional privileges and rights and are bold enough to assert them. They draw their discontent more from a historical sense of discrimination, from the accumulated media image of atrocities against untouchables, and from the observation of untouchability offenses against their fellows, than from a personal experience of untouchability.

Education-cum-government-job and property ownership are two known ways in India for an individual to get local prestige. If a male untouchable is educated, is a government employee, or is literate with some independent source of income (or even merely lives among these kinds of untouchable individuals), he thinks himself worthy of the same prestige and respect as any other baboo. But he does not find it. He enters into a middle class of untouchables, but not into a middle class of India. Thus, the growing Indian middle class in a way has an "ex-untouchable" middle class attached to it, which is still burdened with the stigma of the past. An untouchable sees this reality in a blunt act of untouchability, or in a sophisticated act of discrimination. This modern, liberated soul does not receive what he thinks he deserves. His individual sense of deprivation intensifies when he considers that the same thing has been going on for centuries. His frustration becomes acute with his awareness that his own people, who give him the respect due a baboo, are being treated in inhuman ways in rural areas— a situation he cannot help change.

This frustration is not the result of any particular grievance which might have a certain remedy. An untouchable may fight for his particular right. One might have a problem of promotion, another might try to win proper wages for his fellow village workers. But resolution of particular problems is not likely to result in satisfaction, though it might delay a conflict or an eruption of anger. Their frustration is a general reaction to their overall position in the society.

Untouchables have always been asked to improve themselves to get a better place in the society; Gandhi asked them to keep their houses clean. They think they did so, but where is the promised better place? Though as compared to untouchability in the early twentieth century, when untouchables had to fight for women to be able to cover their breasts, they are better now, they are still not equal in absolute terms. There is no doubt that the social values are not changing as rapidly as the expectations of the untouchables. The administration cannot use its planning preferences and financial allocations to change the values of the society as they can help improve the economic and educational situation of the untouchables. Society is changed by social movements that are not run by the government.

Unfortunately, Indian institutional secularism has not penetrated the hearts of individuals to replace their religious values with the principle of human equality. Even while the nationalist movement promoted a belief in equality, it strengthened its popularity through religious symbolism, reinforcing religion as part of behavior for many. Gandhi himself, though he fought untouchability, did not make the caste system a target of his struggle per se for a major part of his life. After the first generation of national leaders, who made a number of constitutional provisions for the welfare of untouchables, the problem remained merely an issue of politicking.

Today there is no real non-untouchable leadership or movement that can work in society for a value change. Strangely, except for the consensus of national leadership favoring continuing reservations for untouchables, and for a few statements after any massacre of untouchables, no political party or social group comes forward to help, rescue, or heal the wounds of that particular community, much less to work for a longer-range purpose of proper equality among communities.[72] This absence of leadership suggests not only that the process of change in values is very slow, but also that there is no social force accelerating this change within the society. Indeed, there are signs of a weakening political position for untouchables with the rising public opinion against the reservation system. This public opinion is bound to accelerate with the expected strengthening of the backward classes' power, further strengthening the frustrations of untouchables.

The Backward Classes' Rivalry with Untouchables

In the Indian politics of social hierarchy and socio-economic competence, the term "backward classes" is regularly used, defined, and redefined, although it has yet to acquire a definite meaning. This term loosely refers to the Shudra jatis located below the twice-born varnas but above the untouchables.[73]

There is a hundred-year-old governmental practice in India reserving quotas in public services and educational institutions for backward communities. Articles 15(4), 16(4) and 340 of the Indian constitution permit the state to take special measures for the advancement of socially or educationally backward classes. Different castes have been struggling to use these provisions for their advancement. In the arena of national and state politics, the numerical strength of the backward classes has inspired politicians to include them and their issues in their political strategies and manifestos. The much-debated second Backward Classes Commission (Mandal Commission, 1980) appointed by the Janata government was also a result of these dynamics.

The Mandal commission reported that, despite the fact that these classes constitute (by the commission's contested count) 52 percent of the Indian population, they are far behind the scheduled castes and tribes (22.56 percent of the population) in government service jobs.

Scheduled castes and tribes share 18.72 percent of the central government services as compared to the 12.55 percent share of the backward classes.[74] Although these backward classes do not suffer untouchability and have many economic openings other than government jobs, untouchables—due to their governmental privileges—have become a reference group for them. They draw the same parallel in their demand rhetoric as did the Mandal commission.

Backward classes see the relative prosperity of untouchables as gained at the expense of their own opportunities. Where resources are scarce, envy is a natural human reaction.[75] The government is seen as taking sides with the untouchables in this socio-economic competition of communities. The untouchables' progress in government patronage and protection has become one of the government's symbols. And as mobilization for any demand involves an agitational style and a bit of rioting in the current Indian political culture, when the backward castes agitate for their rights, the untouchables become one of the targets of violence, as do public buses, street lights, and police. This violence against untouchables is somewhat different from the classical practice of untouchability. It is a consequence of their competitive strength, not of their subject status. But untouchables count these events as a continuity of the same practices of high caste oppression and, in return, their discontent increases. The backward classes were an important part of the anti-untouchable Maharashtra riots of 1978 and the Gujarat riots of 1981. These riots were against the preferential treatment of untouchables. And violence was directed toward untouchable students and economically better-off individuals of the untouchable community, as I have discussed in an earlier chapter. The Thevars (a "backward class" caste) and untouchables of Tamil Nadu illustrate this pattern of discontent and reactive behavior.

The Case of the Thevars in Tamil Nadu

In Tamil Nadu, Tamil nationalism had the effect of vertically integrating communities, but in recent years it is becoming increasingly clear that some sections of the backward classes have remained far behind the others. Thevars, historically proud of being a martial race, are nowadays in confrontation with the untouchables in the southern districts of Tamil Nadu where they are situated. Tirunelveli,

Ramanathapuram, and Madurai are the districts of recent Thevar/untouchable confrontation and conversion.

Thevar is the common title favored by the kin-castes of Kallar and Maravar. Ritually, Thevars are just above untouchables. Although a few wealthy landlords are found among the Thevars, their economic situation varies from place to place. In Thanjavur, the Kallar tend to live in villages as contract farmers and farm workers. One report notes that in most of their villages, schools are not adequate.[76] The misery and poverty of the ordinary people can be gauged by the emaciated and ill-clad appearance of the boys and girls in the schools. In contrast, in one subdistrict (Madukalathur Taluk in Ramanathapuram District) half of the Maravar people own lands. Comparable data for untouchables and Thevars in education, government jobs, and landownership are not available. However, one government report notes that Thevars have not progressed in education and government employment. There is no evidence of Thevars turning to petty trades or even to business. Nevertheless, Thevars have been a political force in this area because of their number and their old status of relationship to the armies of the rajas. They have normally captured seats in the legislature and in the union. It is safe to say that the Thevars' position is traditionally and politically stronger than that of the untouchables.

Again, the situation may differ from village to village. The chairman of the Backward Class Commission for Tamil Nadu found in two of the villages he visited that, though the majority of the caste community are small landholders, their houses are much worse than the houses of untouchables in the villages. He also found that untouchable boys were very much better dressed and more presentable. He concluded that the majority caste was economically worse off than the untouchables in these villages.[77]

The Thevars feel relative deprivation in comparison with the Tamil Nadu untouchables. Merton explains this phenomenon by placing the concept of relative deprivation in the framework of reference group theory. Relative deprivation is seen as a tendency to define and evaluate one's own position in comparison with a relevant reference group.[78] The Thevars have restlessly watched the Nadars climbing the modern ladder of prestige. They have tried to maintain their traditional control in vain.[79] No wonder that Thevars are now demanding that all the privileges and concessions available to untouchables should be given to them as well.[80] It is an implicit recognition of the economic progress made by the reference group of the adjacent untouchables. Their conflicts are therefore as much a manifestation of this newly acquired discontent as they are a continuity of their old hostility.

In this conflict at the bottom of the society, untouchables have certain disadvantages. They find local administrative apparatus often on the side of the Thevars.

Untouchables' Helplessness in Their Conflict with Thevars

At national and state levels, the system of reservation in parliaments for untouchables ensures their political representation. Untouchables' votes were one of the important factors in the success of the Janata party in 1977 and in the return of the Congress party in 1980. No political party can take untouchables' votes for granted.[81] But despite this relative electoral power they are still handicapped by their ritual status. They do matter in alliances but still cannot play a leading role. In local politics—village level as opposed to state and national level—they face more problems in acquiring power.

In South Asia, local leadership generally emerges either on the basis of traditional advantages as landlord or caste leader and/or is maintained by working for people, using nepotism, links, and clout, through local administration. The image that one is resourceful matters a lot. Caste connections, with political links as well as previous political power, stand as decisive advantages in local politics along with numerical strength. While dominant castes are traditionally used to these manipulations of the local administrative apparatus, untouchables do not normally participate in this kind of local power game of clout formation. Elected representatives help reinforce this clout, as it will in turn strengthen their position. This micro-level influence formation is crucial for an elected representative. But a nominated one, as an untouchable normally is, does not have to go through this process—which he is not in any position to master anyway. Thus, this vicious circle keeps untouchable representation on the periphery of the real game.

The value system which gives the higher castes power to insist on a pattern of behavior from others and to impose their will on them is becoming increasingly unacceptable. Hierarchical exploitation is now difficult to enforce through village *panchayats* (''councils''). In this situation, the dominant caste often uses its political power and its caste-fellow government employees to maneuver the local administrative and police apparatus for its own ends. This is a new tool of coercion, to push untouchables around with indirect punishments and "invisible" troubles. At this local level law and administration is, generally, at the service of political power, i.e., the dominant caste.

The untouchables are not only peripheral to the local informal polity, they are helpless before its power. To a village dweller, "government" means the local police or revenue officer. What can he do if the officer is allied with his enemy? In all the cases of conflict discussed above, untouchables have constantly complained of the partisan anti-untouchable actions of the local police or administrative authorities.[82]

Whenever untouchables assert their rights, they not only have to confront the dominant caste but most of the time they have to face the local government apparatus as well, especially the person who writes the First Information Report. This report is the most crucial document in the Indian judicial system. It is normally written by a low-ranked, semi-ignorant policeman who is subject to all kinds of manipulation, corruption, and the pressures of nepotism. The police officer, in this setting, is not usually the neutral arbiter of social disputes but the armed representative of the communities from which either he was originally recruited, or to whom he is responsive.[83]

In their conflict with the Thevars, untouchables usually find themselves helpless in the presence of a Thevar/police axis.[84] This helplessness further aggravates untouchables' feeling of societal injustice when they find themselves powerless politically. A few untouchables who are included in the cabinet are treated with contempt. There are forty-three members of the Tamil Nadu state assembly who are from untouchable castes. But they are "hand picked by upper caste people to toe their line."[85] The true untouchable leaders are inevitably sidelined.

A Summary of the Analysis

Before discussing the case of conversion, a summary of the previous discussion will be useful.

Modernization and preferential government policies have brought higher levels of consciousness among untouchables in general. These policies have also created a substantial stratum of educated untouchable people, a majority of them economically independent.

Untouchables in Tamil Nadu in particular are economically in a better position than untouchables in other Indian states. But untouchability in Tamil society is still in practice. Untouchables in Tamil Nadu seem more discontented and aggressive than those in many other Indian areas with low socio-economic status and a high level of atrocities.

These changes may vary from village to village. Villages with substantial educated and economically relatively independent untouchable individuals are likely to become more socially mobile than the other villages within Tamil Nadu.

People in this stratum believe that they are rightfully entitled to the equal social status which is being denied them. This discrepancy of value potential and value position is the reason for discontent among them. These people often assert themselves aggressively without any outside inspiration.

Other untouchable people, though not literate or economically independent, also experience relative deprivation, though its nature is less psychological (equality of status) and more material (economic well-being). This is a result of a general increase in communication, higher political consciousness, and socialization with their better-educated untouchable compatriots. These people are susceptible to mobilization by members of the more sensitive stratum described above.

The initiative for change has shifted from the hands of a relatively few known leaders of untouchables to a large number of "ordinary" people who are now willing to confront the system through direct action.

The nature of rebellious behavior also differs from case to case, from individual to collective assertiveness and from physical to psychological violence.

The crucial difference today is the active personal participation of thousands of individuals who are willing to risk confrontations to protest untouchability. Now, untouchables are growing more impatient and less willing to tolerate what they perceive as tokenism.

5

Conversion to Islam

The mass conversion to Islam of a thousand untouchables in Meenakshipuram Village, Tirunelveli District (Tamil Nadu) in February 1981 has been treated as the event that triggered the conversion movement in Tamil Nadu. This is correct as far as the national debate is concerned, but the first major conversion to Islam occurred in Kurayoor (Madurai) in 1979. According to the chief minister of Tamil Nadu, there were cases of conversion almost every year in the period 1969-78.[86] One Muslim leader in Madras estimated that in recent years two to three thousand people per year have converted to Islam. The total number of converts, however, is a matter of dispute. The highest number given is thirty-two thousand. One computation based on the Indian national press suggests a total of 2,873 converts and 17,200 who threatened to convert in Tamil Nadu, during the seven months of 1981.[87] But I have found that many villages were never reported on in the press. The exact figures are difficult to determine. Muslim organizations of Tamil Nadu usually either do not reply to this question, or tend to minimize the figures; some even say they do not keep any numerical record. Nevertheless, it is probably safe to conclude that there were no more than twelve thousand conversions during the 1979-1981 period.

This study will mainly include data from the following villages of Tamil Nadu:

Village	Taluka	District	Number of Converts
Ettivayal	Paramakudi	Ramanathapuram	150
Kandai	Tirumangalam	Madurai	285
Kooriyoor	Ramanathapuram	Ramanathapuram	328
Kurayur	Tirumangalam	Madurai	280
Veeravanur	Paramakudi	Ramanathapuram	150
Meenakshipuram	Tenkasi	Tirunelveli	1,100

Meenakshipuram Village is not found in the 1971 census report. However, government and press reports provide a great deal of qualitative information and some figures, enough for a comparative analysis. Conversion in all the above-mentioned villages occurred in 1980-81.

Press and government reports vary on the number of converts by village. Sometimes homonymous names have also created a problem, for example Kurayoor/Kurayur/Kuriyur/Kooriyur or Ilamanur/Elamor. The name of the taluka (''sub-district'') of the village is also not mentioned in these reports. This makes it difficult to identify the village. For this reason I could not include Ilamanoor, a village of 550 converts. I have also selected only those villages for my data base which have more than 100 converts, as they provide a more reliable base for generalization. Many villages account for between twenty to sixty converts each, spreading over four districts of Tamil Nadu: Ramanathapuram, Madurai, Tirunelveli and Thanjavur. I had to leave out Sakkudirb Village (480 converts) because I could not find any mention of this village in the national press, though it was reported by converts and by Muslim organizations.

What Kinds of Villages Are These?

These villages have a much larger-than-average portion of untouchable population, a below-average number of agricultural laborers, and a variable rate of literacy as compared to Tamil Nadu's overall percentages (see Table 6).

The percentages of agricultural laborers given in column 5 of Table 6 are of the total population, which shows a below-average number of agricultural laborers in these villages. Of the total rural agricultural laborers in Tamil Nadu, 43.48 percent are untouchables. Therefore, the proportion of untouchable laborers may be even lower, as the

Table 6

Socio-Economic Conditions of Untouchables in the Villages of Conversion Compared with Tamil Nadu Data

1	2	3	4	5	6	7	8	9
Place	Population	Percentage of Literates Among Total Rural Males	No. of Rural Agricultural Laborers	Percentage of Rural Agricultural Laborers to the Total Rural Workers	No. of Persons Belonging to Untouchable Castes	Percentage of Untouchables in Rural Population	No. of Untouchable Rural Agricultural Laborers[1]	Percentage of Rural Untouchable Population Who Are Agricultural Laborers[2]
Tamil Nadu	41,199,168	45.14%	4,180,735	38.09%	7,315,595	21.06%	1,809,403	29.90%
Ettivayal	1,068	53.11%	41	11.74%	427	39.98%	18	4.15%
Kandai	670	45.02%	82	25.07%	474	70.74%	35	7.49%
Kooriyoor	1,197	36.31%	46	12.53%	621	51.87%	20	3.21%
Kurayur	4,039	52.72%	762	39.44%	1,171	28.99%	330	28.16%
Veeravanur (a/a + a/b)	2,172	44.99%	211	22.11%	947	43.60%	91	9.64%

Sources: Calculations are based upon the data in: *Census of India 1971,* Series 19, Tamil Nadu Part II-C-1, pp. 66-7; *Census of India 1971,* Series 1, part II-C (ii), p. 146; *Census of India 1971,* Series 19, Part II A, p. 319; *Census of India 1971,* Series 19, Part X-B, *District Census Handbook, Ramanathapuram District,* Volume I, pp. 404-7, 438-41; *Census of India 1971,* Series 19, Part X-B, *District Census Handbook, Madurai District,* Volume II, pp. 870-3, 862-5.

Notes: The term used for untouchables in the census reports is Scheduled Castes.

[1] Numbers of untouchable agricultural laborers by village are not available in census reports. I have calculated these numbers from the numbers of agricultural laborers in respective villages on the basis of available information that 43.28% of the total rural agricultural laborers in Tamil Nadu are untouchables. Therefore actual numbers may be higher or lower. Numbers given are rounded.

[2] These figures are based upon above-mentioned assumption in Note 1.

calculation in column 9 of Table 6 shows. The qualitative data discussed later in this paper depict a better economic condition of untouchables in these villages. However, if one assumes that all of these agricultural laborers are untouchables, which is unlikely, even then only 9.60 percent, 17.37 percent, 7.40 percent, 65.07 percent, and 22.28 percent respectively of the untouchable population of these villages would be considered agricultural laborers, calculating on the bases of column 4 and 6 of Table 6. These percentages demonstrate that the conversion villages must have fewer untouchable agricultural laborers than the Tamil Nadu average of 29.90 percent of the untouchable population. Only Kurayur's situation is different. However, our qualitative information categorically denies that all the untouchables in these villages are agricultural laborers.

The untouchable literacy rate is difficult to determine in these villages. The general rural male literacy rate in Tamil Nadu is 45.14 percent, while the untouchable rural male literacy rate is 29.39 percent. However, the village figures could at least be analyzed as follows: that an untouchable population higher than the state average is not exercising a negative effect on the literacy rate by depressing the percentage below the Tamil Nadu rate in these villages. This indicates that the gap between general and untouchable literacy rates found in Tamil Nadu does not exist in these villages, although they have a higher population of untouchables. This is confirmed by newspaper reports that suggest that untouchables in these villages have the same, if not a better, literacy rate than caste Hindus.

Although census data are not found on Meenakshipuram, the information available in newspapers and in the report of the director of scheduled castes presents the same image of Meenakshipuram as of the villages discussed above. Meenakshipuram is an 82.95 percent untouchable village, though the surrounding villages are predominantly caste villages. Most of the village dwellers are registered as cultivating tenants. It has a good number of employed untouchables, including twenty-six graduates; one of these is district agricultural officer and another district superintendent officer, four are doctors, seven trained teachers, and one is an engineer.[88] More than 40 percent of the untouchables are educated. Eighty families out of 180 own land, and the biggest landholder in the village is an untouchable.[89]

Each of these villages, including Meenakshipuram, has one to three primary schools: one village even has a middle school. All have drinking water facilities. Three of them did not have electricity in 1971,

but now all do. All have village post offices. A medical facility was,
however, available only in Kurayur, according to the 1971 census.

These data are from 1971, while the events which we are discussing
took place ten years later. Presumably these observed trends must have
strengthened by 1980-81, when the conversions took place. Tamil Nadu
reported an enrollment ratio of 115.3 percent of untouchable students to
the general population in the corresponding age group in primary classes
in the year 1977-78. This is not a sudden change, it is a trend. Primary
classes during 1973-74 and 1974-75 had 93.4 percent and 91.6 percent
enrollment of untouchables,[90] which suggests that almost all untouchable
teenagers have had some school even if they are not functionally literate.
Considering the relative advantages of these conversion villages, one can
imagine that they might have performed even better than the Tamil
Nadu averages. This may be the basis of one press reporter's conclusion that 80 percent of the Kooriyoor population is educated.

Although the low percentage of agricultural laborers suggests that
the untouchables in these villages are economically independent, it is
possible that their independence is merely nominal. They might have a
little land. They may not have access to credit, or they may be in debt.
The data are insufficient to measure the factual economic situation.
But all the eyewitness assessments in the press maintain that untouchables in these villages are in a better economic position than in many
other villages, and that untouchables' prosperity is almost the same as
that of many non-untouchables. More important, the poor untouchables are not poorer than the other poor people.[91] Although Kurayur
like other villages is divided by a road that separates caste and non-
caste populations, there is hardly any visible difference in the life style
of the two groups.[92] Almost all untouchables in Kurayur have she-
buffalos and the government dairy service collects milk from this village
on a daily basis. Similar economic conditions have been reported by those
who have visited Meenakshipuram. "The village looks prosperous,"
observed a news reporter.[93]

The Socio-Economic Position
of Converts and Their Leaders

Press reports show that the typical characteristics of these villages
are also prominent among the new Muslims. Such reports indicate that

educated untouchable individuals have acted as leaders of conversion in their localities. At least five are doctors, among them one in Kurayur, one in Kooriyoor and two in Meenakshipuram.[94] Wardha Nagar's (Tamil Nadu) municipal health officer, Dr. Mohan, also became "Dr. Muhammad."[95] A few police constables, sub-inspectors of police, civil employees and one IAS officer are also among the conversion leaders. In Kooriyoor, an untouchable trustee of the Ramanathapuram Temple (one of the five holiest shrines in India) has embraced Islam. An untouchable reporter for *Malai Murasu*, a Tamil daily, converted to Islam in Allinagaram (Theni) in Madurai District. New Muslims also include one lawyer, Muhammad Khalid, and one ex-member of the legislative assembly, C.M. Ambikapathy (now Abdul Hadi) of Thanjavur District (Hammanupatti Village). The Ramanathapuram Taluka secretary of the ADMK, Mr. Dinakaran (now Muhammad Ismail), has also opted for Islam.

A public audit clerk in Meenakshipuram became the first in his area to put the option of conversion before his fellows. In Kooriyoor, initiative was taken by the Madurai-based lawyer who hails from that village and has land there. In Kandai, the initiator of conversions has land in the village but lives outside it, where he works as a carpenter—a trade he learned in school. In Thanjavur District there was a former member of the legislative assembly (mentioned above) who was the motivator. The professions and occupations of these and the other individuals mentioned clearly suggest that they not only belonged to the elite of untouchables, but that they were socially and spatially mobile. All of them were well-educated and economically well off. They were not caste leaders, but they were accepted as opinion leaders by their fellows. These leaders or semi-leaders of conversion were mostly government employees and probably found their way up through the government's reservation system.[96] With one exception, all the leaders of the conversion movement were below forty years of age.

Perception of Government Policies

None of the new converts interviewed believed that the government's reservation policies are insufficient or inaccessible. The *Meenakshipuram Report* of the director of scheduled castes also specified that the village was benefiting from the grants of stipends, scholarships,

government-supplied drinking water facilities, and electricity. None of
the converts in the extensive press reports complained of the government's policies. However, some respondents, mostly non-converts and
those who threatened to convert, deplored the inaccessibility of governmental programs. The converts' approval of reservation programs
may be either because most of them did receive some of the government's benefits, or simply because they did not attach much importance to the government programs. At any rate, activists among new
Muslims have taken the stand that government programs and reform-
ist statements are a variety of tokenism. I think that this attitude has its
basis in the relative irrelevance of the issue to this stratum, as they are
economically better off than the rest. A majority of them, however, did
mention as a cost of equality, loss of these benefits following conversion. The greater concern for equality seems to have outweighed the
subsequent inaccessibility of government programs. Muhammad You-
suf, a high school dropout, quoted his reply to a government officer
who asked him why he decided to relinquish all the help which the
government gives untouchables:

> You are right that government has done many things for us. It has been
> kind, but did you not see that wealthy people love to keep dogs as pets?
> They provide good food...and every comfort...to them, but Sir! If
> someone will ask, who is he, what will one reply! Of course, a dog. So
> that is our position. You are giving us facilities, but what is the use of
> those programmes which can fill the stomach without making one a
> human being?[97]

The comment of Meenakshipuram's headman who did not convert,
though he sympathizes with new Muslims, is in an idiom of bitterness
about the achievements of reform: "The word *Harijan* is not even as
respectable as that four letter word...."[98] (Harijan is the name intro-
duced by Gandhi for untouchables, meaning "children of God.")

This indifference may be because they have become used to the
government program. Or, psychologically, they are less impressed and
less likely to reciprocate favors if they believe that the others have no
choice in helping them.[99]

Perception of Relative Deprivation

The new converts think that equal treatment is their due but is
being denied to them. One, Syed Muhammad, puts his perception of

relative deprivation in comparison with other groups: "Whenever *we* open a shop, caste Hindus do not buy anything from *our* shop, while Muslims do. Are not we Hindus? *We* are physically fit and educationally equal. Why are *we being treated* badly?" (Interview, emphasis added.) The economic aspect of the problem is more evident in this comment, but the contrast between their improved educational and economic position and the unequal treatment the society metes out to them was one of the most common and oft-repeated arguments put forth by the converts in justifying their anger.

One scholar, who studied two villages where conversion took place, says about Kandai that untouchables in their village, where they form the majority, are "very much their own masters." But "they must take off their *chappals* ("slippers") in Thevar villages and get down from their bicycles." One of his respondents told him of the remark a local Thevar made only a week before they met as he was going past his field where he was working, "You Pallar fellow, you have your lands, but that does not make you our equal, don't think that." One politically active untouchable told his story: "When campaigning politically a few years ago, he had been canvassing for the Congress. He had been traveling in the car belonging to the congress local leaders, but even then he had been ordered to get out and walk when he came to a Thevar village."[100] The same discrepancies between the acquired educational and economic position of untouchables and their denied social status have been attested in almost all the reports exploring the causes of conversion in relevant villages. This situation is the basis of frustration and discontent among the untouchables.

Thevar/Police Axis Against the Untouchables

There are plenty of sound examples of untouchability discrimination in the villages under study. Meenakshipuram untouchables were served by a different barber and in a separate place, but nonetheless, Thevars made this barber close his service. Outside their village, they were served tea in coconut shells instead of regular cups available for caste customers. Even the untouchables' own village teashop was pulled down by Thevars.[101] These are clear foundations for registering cases under the Protection of the Civil Rights Act. Other conversion villages have the same kind of problem. In Kandai, the Thevars often

allow their sheep, cows, and other animals to wander into the untouchables' lands to find fodder.[102]

One may ask why untouchables in these villages, as educated as
they are, do not try to take legal action. But it is not easy for untouchables to resort to the legal administrative apparatus. In the countryside, police are more responsive to the dominant caste than to the
untouchables. In many cases, they themselves come from the dominant caste. Therefore, an untouchable might observe, "How can I
complain to the police who themselves helped Thevars to pull down
my teashop in Meenakshipuram?"[103] Kandai untouchables also maintain that even if they report such things to the police, nothing happens.[104] The police are hardly impartial authorities in these areas of
conversion. One sociological inquiry also observes that "the Thevar
officers are reported to be the worst enemies of the Harijans." The role
of the additional inspector general of police at the time, a Thevar, and
that of a number of other police and revenue officers belonging to the
Thevar caste, has become controversial and questionable.[105] Whatever
untouchable police officers are given duty in the area are "managed"
not to stay long.[106] As mentioned before, the director of scheduled
castes' report on the Meenakshipuram conversions is a good account
of how Thevar—a dominant caste in the area—maneuvered police to
harass untouchables because one untouchable married a Thevar girl.
Many who have studied conversion in Meenakshipuram believe that
untouchables' prolonged conflict with Thevars and police culminated
in conversion when police started raiding untouchables' houses,[107]
i.e., violence and the discriminatory administration of justice triggered
the response.

Different Ways to Conversion

A common fallacy in the debate following the Meenakshipuram
conversions has been that all subsequent cases were caused by a domino
effect from Meenakshipuram. It has already been noted that Meenakshipuram was not the first case. Meenakshipuram did have an impact, but
different villages had a momentum and leaders of their own, which led to
their conversion. Unfortunately, insufficient information is available
about the process of conversion in the five villages whose socio-economic
data I have analyzed. However, enough information about at least four

localities is available, three from our set of villages. They differ in their method of conversion, in intensity of aggression and in the spontaneity of events.

Meenakshipuram

In this case, the news was reported as though it were a very strange and unexpected event. The director of scheduled castes in Tamil Nadu cited new converts as saying that

> ...their elders were thinking of converting to Islam for the last twenty years. They have been having this idea time and again. Since there was no support and unanimity three times earlier, they did not convert. This is the fourth time when a good number of them came forward to get converted.[108]

Concluding his report, the director supported this statement with the results of his confidential inquiries from some of the nonconverted untouchables who revealed that the Harijans of the village took the initiative.[109] But there also had been a history of untouchable assertiveness, of Thevars' oppressive treatment, and of conflict in which the police supported the Thevars. The murder of two Thevars in December 1980 (two months before the conversion) brought a new wave of police torture and harassment for the untouchables of the village. This situation caused untouchables to adopt a collective strategy. Thus, in a village gathering, they resolved to convert in response to a proposal by one of the young men who had converted to Islam earlier. Their exposure to Islam was mainly through social contact with the Muslims of the area, who had been a political power in this electoral constituency for at least forty years. This conversion came as a collective decision of converts, albeit in three installments.

Kooriyoor

Here the initiative was taken first by a new Muslim, Muhammad Khalid, a Madurai-based lawyer. He was sent to prison by the police on trumped-up charges (as he characterizes it). In prison he decided to convert to Islam. The day after his release he came to his village and announced his decision. Khalid's decision was a spontaneous reaction, though prior thought and familiarity with Muslims were in the background. He started preaching in his village and surroundings. He says that within twenty days, fifty-two people in his village had accepted

Islam. In December 1981, two-and-a-half years after his conversion, the total number of new Muslims in his village reached 328, half of the total untouchable community. This slow pace shows that in Kooriyoor, conversion was an individual rather than a collective decision. As Khalid himself asserts: "I can bring ten thousand people into Islam within days but I want everyone to come by himself after understanding it, by his own personal choice...."[110]

It may be, considering the low proportion of agricultural laborers, that people in this village are more individualistic in their life styles, more capable, and more in the habit of making their own decisions than less-sophisticated rural types. The Muslim organization with which this village came into contact is the Tablighi Jama'at, a loosely organized Islamic religious movement with a small presence in Tamil Nadu. Conversion in this village did not come in a ceremonial style, as it did in Meenakshipuram.

Kandai

The direct evangelism of two brothers, who were from Kandai but had gone elsewhere to work, seems to have been responsible for conversion in this village. They met some Muslims in a teashop, and through them learned the process of conversion. In addition, some untouchables in this village have marriage ties with the villages where conversion had taken place. They were aware of conversion in Meenakshipuram and Kurayur. No particular incident, such as police torture or a clash with Thevars, was reported as an immediate cause of conversion in this village. Leaders of the Muslim Center in Madurai were brought to the village for the conversion ceremony.[111] Conversion in this village may possibly have been the result of a domino effect from other conversions.

Villages of Thanjavur

In three villages of Thanjavur District—Ekkal, Kunnaloor, and Thirutharaipundi—300 untouchables changed their faith to Islam. The influential personality in this region was a former member of the legislative assembly, Abdul Hadi. He says, "I was not converted, I embraced Islam in its literal sense.... A political life spanning over three decades and study of Islam for over twenty months led me to this...faith."[112] His statement makes it evident that he was influenced by Islamic literature, produced by Jama'at-e-Islami. He recited *Kalima* (declaration of belief in one God and in His human messenger Muhammad) by himself, saying in a peculiarly anti-clerical tone, "[I]n Islam we do not need anyone else to make us Muslim." While Abdul Hadi was still studying Islam, his brother, Hariharn, who happens to be the father-in-law of T.M. Karunanidhi, a sitting member of *Lok Sabha* (Indian parliament, 1981), took the lead in embracing Islam, and all his family members including his grandchildren became Muslim. He preaches Islam by giving Islamic books to others. His conversion, then, was a mature leader's inner decision to leave his ancestors' faith. The option for the other faith was influenced by the Islamic literature, though social contact with Muslims was also a factor.

There are few common features in these four instances of conversion. In two villages there was conflict immediately before conversion, but not in the other two. Leaders of conversion in three villages had social contacts with Muslims while one did not. Only two of them had been thinking about conversion for some time.

The Ceremony of Conversion

Most of the converts recited *Kalima*, individually or in a small group to become Muslim. But in some villages it was in large numbers and in the form of a ceremony. One social scientist, Andrew Wingate, was present at such a ceremony in Kandai. His account is typical of other conversion ceremonies. The ceremony began with a sermon, preached by one of the leaders of the Muslim Center in Madurai. It had three main points—one theological, one social, and one economic:

> If they joined Islam, they must put away all other gods and idols, Allah alone would be their God. If they joined Islam they must forget their previous caste. They would be no longer Pallars, but Muslims, just as Nadars were no longer Nadars, but Muslims. If they joined Islam, they should not expect any economic miracles, or believe any stories about Arab money pouring in for them. They should see the houses of the people who had joined earlier; they had received no economic benefit. They can come up in future only by hard work and discipline.

After the sermon followed the *Kalima*, in which the resident imam of the village, unlike a Christian pastor, did not take the major part. Each new Muslim was admitted by a different Muslim, who helped

him recite *Kalima*. Next he was given a Muslim name and a new hat.
He was then embraced by a number of old Muslims. The process was
repeated for the next man. At the end, combined worship was held,
followed by a common meal. Old and new Muslims sat together side
by side and exchanged some food from each other's plates, using their
hands, as a symbol of fellowship. After depicting the ceremony the
author wrote:

> ...the discipline, cleanliness, and care in teaching of the Mullahs, the
> way they mingle with the people, and the clarity of their dogmatic
> teaching, does have an attraction, at least at first, for these village peo-
> ple. So too does the sight of a new congregation bowing in unison and
> silence, to Allah, in the open view of all in the village, in a tent-
> mosque.[113]

Social Contact with Muslims

Certain scattered references on the untouchable/Muslim relationship are found in the literature. The commissioner of scheduled castes
observes that in the villages where untouchables are completely barred
from fetching water from public places, they are at the mercy of "other
communities for getting drinking water."[114] This term, *other communities*," probably means other religious communities, as the common
Indian usage suggests. This extreme situation is found in about 10 percent of Indian villages. In the other 85 percent of the Indian villages
which have a relatively less severe untouchability water-exclusion policy, the alternate source of water is also available to individuals who
have an occasional problem of this kind. (Only 5 percent of the villages
do not have any problem, as discussed in Chapter 2.) There are some
other reports which note the general availability of this "other community option" for untouchables in some other matters, such as laun-
dry and hair-dressing services, as well.

Muslim business in Tamil Nadu is another area of social contact.
Tanneries were once a Muslim monopoly; whereas ownership of tanneries is still Muslim-dominated, the employees are predominantly
untouchables. The same is the case with concerns manufacturing *beedi*
("inexpensive cigarettes"). In some other trades and commerce also,
untouchables are employed by Muslims. In at least three cases, converts have mentioned Muslim employers' attitudes with admiration.
An Elamannoor shop employee said, "I have closely observed Muslims

while working in a Muslim's shop. I found their company an enjoyable one. I never had the contemptuous treatment at their hands which was common with my erstwhile co-religionists.'' In Vanumbadi, sixty formerly untouchable employees of a Muslim tannery mentioned the friendly attitude and the commensality practices of Muslim employers as a reason for their conversion.

6

Tamil Muslims

In order to understand the Tamil Nadu conversions to Islam, we need to consider not only the social and economic condition of the untouchables, as we have done until now, but also the position of Muslims within the Indian society. This position differs in significant ways between north and south. Tamil Muslims' different characteristics have particular effects on the outlooks and options of untouchables. Culturally, Tamil Muslims differ from what is considered the North Indian cultural tradition of Indian Muslims, who still treat the Urdu language and similar cultural characteristics almost as aspects of their religious identity. Tamil Muslims rather resemble the Muslims of Bengal, of Kerala in India, and of the Sind and North West Frontier Province in Pakistan, who retained their "little traditions" as well.[115] The source of their Islamic faith has little to do with the culture of Muslims in northern states. Because of their external or peripheral relationship to the northern Muslim empires, Tamil Muslims' identification with greater Muslim tradition did not result in linguo-cultural domination by northern Muslims. Furthermore, they benefited from an independent link to other sources of Islamic education. In Tamil Nadu, Kerala, and Sind, it was the Arab world; in the case of the frontier province, it was central Asia itself.

Tamil Muslims do not think themselves alien to Tamil Nadu, nor do they view themselves as members of a displaced North Indian Muslim community.[116] Historically, like Muslims in Malabar, Tamil Muslims attribute their faith to the preachings of the Arab traders of the early Islamic era (seventh century AD). Until the Malik Kafur invasion from the north in AD 1312, the Muslim community in Tamil Nadu had no contact with the northern empires. Tamil Muslim intellectuals point out that Muslim soldiers of the Pandya Kingdom in South India refused to ally with Malik Kafur and fought against him. Even his Muslim rule at Madurai did not last more than fifty years.[117] Later, in the eighteenth century, southern Muslims under the fabled Tipu Sultan tried for political independence. The Qutabshahi kings of Golkonda (1512-1687) and the Nizams of Hyderabad after 1707 also could not reach the far south constituted by Tamil Nadu, Kerala and most of Karnataka. Thus not only is the period of northern political dominance limited, but the Tamil Muslims do not have a history of cultural political domination.

Tamil Muslims are largely Tamil speakers. The census report of 1891 notes: "The Muhammadans of this presidency are mostly of Dravidian origin. The majority retain the vernacular of their ancestors. . . Tamil."[118] However, in the northern districts of Tamil Nadu, Muslims are bilingual. They speak Urdu as well as Tamil, whereas in the southern districts Muslims are exclusively Tamil-speaking.[119]

The majority of Tamil Muslims follow *Shafei fiqh* (one of the five established schools of Islamic jurisprudence). Tamil Nadu is the only region where the Shafei school of the Islamic tradition is found in India, most of which follow *Hanafi fiqh*. The presence of this school suggests the extent of the direct Tamil contact with Arab culture and its resulting influence. *Fiqh* literally means "understanding" in Arabic. This discipline of Islamic knowledge, studied in Islamic seminaries all over the world, discusses the proper answers to questions of legal and personal practice in the light of the *Quran* (revelations made by God to prophet Muhammad, on him be peace) and *Sunnah* (practices of the prophet). Hanafi and Shafei are the two most followed schools of fiqh in the Muslim world today. They are named after their founding scholars. These schools are not separate churches or sects. Their differences are methodological in nature, resulting in divergence of opinion on some of the details of Islamic law. Imam Hanafi's principles of Islamic jurisprudence give greater importance to *qiyas* ("rational analogy") than the Shafei's. The Shafei, on the other hand, emphasize the Quran and Sunnah. From this closer reference to Quran and Sunnah follows a greater simplicity at the level of religious practices, and a continued interest in reading these texts among the followers of Shafei. Although Tamil has a quite different script, almost all Muslim students learn to read the Quran in Arabic.

There is a strong tendency among Tamil Muslims to refer to the *Quran*. In Madras one often hears of Muslim preoccupation with real estate. One RSS (Rashtriya Swayamsevak Sangh, a Hindu extremist organization) pamphlet even said that Muslims have already bought one-half of Madras. This statement reflects upon the fact that Muslims avoid depositing their savings in banks due to the involvement of interest, which is prohibited by the *Quran*. Therefore, they prefer investing their savings in real estate. Mattison Mines notes, as evidence of the same trait among Tamil Muslims: "Muslims. . . believe that conducting business is a *Sunnah* and is, therefore, an occupation conveying religious merit."[120] However, one should not miss the sociological factors behind this preoccupation with trade and business: that these Tamils were influenced by the Arab traders and continued in the same pattern of occupation. This greater religiosity, plus their contact with Arab simplicity, are largely responsible for the egalitarianism of Tamil Muslim society.

The Islamicity of Tamil Muslims is reinforced by revivalist tendencies and literature. One researcher observed about Sri Lankan Muslims as early as 1974 that "the college-trained *maulavis* ("religious scholars") who teach in regular government schools nowadays present a more uniform and modern approach to Islam using textbooks written in Tamil."[121] He thinks that this has resulted in "religious reforms and increased pan-Islamic consciousness." The known close contact between Indian and Sri Lankan Tamils raises the probability of the penetration of revivalist tendencies and literature to the nearby Tamil-speaking Muslim brothers.

The Tamil Muslim identity has two elements in it, linguo-cultural solidarity with Tamil Nadu and a greater Muslim brotherhood at large springing from the Islamicity of Tamils. Both the identities survive side by side, and are manifest in the political arena as well. Tamil Muslims supported the Khilafat movement, as other Indian Muslims did, and backed Dravidian nationalism, as other Tamils did.[122] This dual identity is the reason that Srinivasa Aiyangar, though bitter otherwise about Muslims, wrote, "the Musalaman who had learnt to live on friendly terms with the Hindus. . . have also in a way affected, though in an imperceptible degree, the Dravidian life and thought."[123]

Economically, Tamil Muslims are a relatively prosperous community. The literature on Tamil Nadu does not provide much information on Tamil Muslims, but even if a book contains no more than one or two lines on Tamil Muslims, they concern their supposed preoccupation with trade and business.[124] This general image must be a major attribute of the position of Muslims in the society.

As mentioned above, the hides and skins industry used to be a Muslim monopoly. Tamil Nadu was at one time one of the largest exporters of leather in the world. Muslims still own many concerns and export houses. Despite its association with ritual pollution, in the past two decades Hindus have moved into this field on the ownership and managerial levels. But Muslims and low-caste Hindus continue to monopolize the other levels of the industry. Muslims—as noted—have been prominent in beedi manufacturing in Tamil Nadu, and they own the largest concerns.[125]

Muslims, like other Tamils, have also been in contact with Sri Lanka and other Southeast Asian countries. These contacts are still alive, and are of three types: those of laborers, migrant businessmen, and of exporters from Tamil Nadu. Several Muslim merchants have conducted businesses overseas in Ceylon (now Sri Lanka), Burma, and other Southeast Asian countries. This overseas income was generally reinvested by this business-oriented community in trade and commerce.[126] A survey shows that, unlike the Hindus, who invest in agricultural land, Tamil Muslims make reinvestment their highest priority. Business stands as the second highest priority even among those Tamil Muslims who are not in business, whether urban or rural.[127]

Educational Institutions

Muslims have also used this overseas income to build educational institutions. The Indian government after independence put a ban on government-supported communal schools. The Muslims of Tamil Nadu in response embarked on opening schools and colleges of their own. There were eleven Muslim colleges in 1973, four of which were founded in the fifties, three in the sixties, and two in 1971. All of these are exclusively founded and wholly managed by Muslims, but are open to all the communities. Non-Muslims, therefore, form the majority (53.56 percent) of the students and staff.[128] Tamil Muslims in Burma,

Malaysia, Ceylon, and Vietnam were the main financial base for the first three colleges. All other colleges are financed by Muslim business-men within Tamil Nadu.[129] Considering Tamil Muslims' religiosity, one can imagine the *zakat* money[130] also flowing into this educational activity which, including schools, involved 116 institutions in 1973. Here it will be advisable to discuss zakat in some detail.

Zakat literally means "growth and purification" in Arabic. It is the third pillar of Islam. Every Muslim possessing more than a certain amount of wealth is obliged to give two and a half percent of it each year as the welfare due. *Zakat* is frequently mentioned in the Quran along with the duty of prayers. The Quran considers it a claim of the poor on the wealth of the rich.[131] The collection and distribution of *zakat* is the responsibility of the Islamic state. Today, however, hardly any Muslim country, with the exception of Pakistan and probably Saudi Arabia, dis-charges this responsibility. Instead, it is nowadays mainly paid either to an array of Islamic organizations and institutions who use it for the build-ing and maintenance of free educational institutions, boarding houses, clinics, and orphanages, or it is dispersed personally to deserving individ-uals. *Zakat*, however, cannot be used for mosques.[132] Students and edu-cational institutions have been considered legitimate recipients by Islamic jurists, and have remained among the major beneficiaries of *zakat*. Tamil Muslims, it seems, have used this provision to its best advantage.

Economic Position

The evidence about Tamil Muslims' preoccupation with trade and business corroborates the general image of Muslims in Tamil Nadu. But the question remains, how prosperous are the Tamil Nadu Mus-lims really? This question becomes more important in light of their being considered a backward community in the official categories. These categories, however, sometimes reflect the bargaining power and political clout of a community. The 1970 Tamil Nadu *Report on Backward Classes* is vague about the evaluation of the Muslims' eco-nomic position. It says that some families have taken to trade and busi-ness in recent decades. The report counts cultivation, ferrying, manual labor, betel-leaf selling, and tailoring among their occupations. Muslims have taken to practically all the professions of the backward classes, from weaving and net-weaving to fishing.[133]

No data except the population figures for Muslims are available in the Indian census reports to determine the general socio-economic position of Muslims. Therefore, this study has used the unobtrusive measure of advertisements in the newspapers to analyze the Muslims' position as consumers. Assuming that advertisements in the newspapers reflect the buying power of consumers in the society, the number of advertisements have been counted and the space has been measured which is used to appeal to the Muslim consumer on the day of *Eid* (the most important Muslim festival throughout the world, on which adherents spend the most). The news reports about Eid celebrations in the same newspapers have also been taken into account.[134] This method will help to infer the Tamil Muslims' economic condition, compared to the condition of Muslims living in other parts of India (see Table 7). As will be apparent, the Madras paper carries a much higher proportion of Eid advertisements than do North Indian papers.

Tamil Nadu's newspaper, *The Hindu*, is the only paper which has advertisements of two financial institutions and one of the Lions Club, appealing to Muslims, pointing to both the economic and social position of Tamil Muslims.[135] Tamil Nadu was also the only region where restaurants and food products were advertised to attract Muslim consumers on the consumption-oriented Eid day. In total, five times as much space was used to attract Muslim consumers in Tamil Nadu as in the three northern-based newspapers, which have the majority of Muslim readers, combined. Our comparison clearly establishes the strong purchasing power of the Muslims in Tamil Nadu. Muslims' preoccupation with business in Madras, however, might have made them decide to place the advertisements themselves, but there is no evidence to support this probability.

Muslims have a comparatively high degree of urbanization in Tamil Nadu. Approximately 55 percent live in cities and towns.[136] In contrast, Muslims have a low level of literacy in the state. Literacy data on the basis of religion are not published in the census reports, but one government report of 1970 notes that: "literacy among Muslims...cannot in any sense be said to exceed 10 to 20 percent of their population in Tamil Nadu."[137]

So much for the relatively better economic position of the Tamil Muslims. As far as government services are concerned, Tamil Muslims formed 3.33 percent of the Madras Civil Service (executive branch), according to available figures. Although it is less than their proportion of 5.11 percent in the Tamil Nadu population, it is far better than

Table 7

Analysis of Newspaper Advertisements
Reflecting Muslims' Economic Position in Different Regions of India

City of Publication	Name of Newspaper	News Item on Eid	Total No. of Advertisements in Newspaper	No. of Advertisements Aimed at Muslim Consumer*	Total Space of Advertisements for Muslim Consumer, in Inches	Themes of These Advertisements
Calcutta	Statesman	No	112	2	50.6''	Products
Delhi	Indian Express	No	78	4	23.6''	Films
Delhi	Hindustan Times	No	149	None**	––	––
Bombay	Times of India	Yes	197	10	149.1''	7 Films, 2 Personal, 1 Company
Madras	Hindu	Yes	130	16+***	361.3''	7 Films, 4 Food and Restaurants, 2 Banks, 1 Product, 1 Company, 1 Lions Club

Note: All the newspapers examined here are of July 23, 1982.

* I have counted advertisements bearing Eid greetings in this category.

** But it does include a 1½'' greeting from the paper.

*** Seven other advertisements covering 175.81'' also seem to be directed towards the "celebrating readers" but do not explicitly use words for Eid greetings.

Muslims' representation at the all-India level in the Indian Administrative Service, where Muslims are 2.9 percent of total officers, contrasted to their proportion of 11.21 percent in the Indian population. (The proportion at central government level will go down to 1.61 percent if all Class 1—executive cadre—employees are counted.)[138] Therefore, it is safe to say that Tamil Muslims are ahead of other Indian Muslims in their share of the government services—a source of prestige and economic welfare which can occasionally be used, by some, for the help of one's community in India.

Castelessness of Tamil Muslims

Tamil Muslims are often called *Labbai*. This is the term used for Tamil-speaking Muslims in the census report of 1921 and earlier, as distinguished from the Urdu-speaking Muslims. In practice, all Tamil Nadu government departments now consider every Muslim who speaks some Tamil *Labbai*.[139] This term does not refer to any single caste, community, or specific occupation.[140] However, Mines' study does name four "subdivisions" among Tamil Muslims: Labbai, Rawther, Marakayar, and Kayalar, but his objective conclusion about their "casteness" is the same as the Tamil Muslims' subjective assertion that these are not castes.[141] Mines says:

> All four sub-divisions are of approximately equal status. Status sociograms, movable card ranking and observations of interaction among members of different subdivisions reveal that, unlike Hindu castes, the Muslim subdivisions are not ranked...but ranking exists on the level of the individual and is based primarily on the individual's conduct, his age, wealth, personal character and religiousness.[142]

Imtiaz Ahmad, however, does not accept Mines' thesis and suspects that the evidence presented by him does not completely rule out the presence of hierarchical ranking and caste considerations among the Tamil Muslims.[143] As no other in-depth sociological study is available regarding caste among Muslims in Tamil Nadu, the works on Tamil Muslims of Sri Lanka have been looked into to evaluate the validity of Mines's generalizations based on his work in one Tamil Nadu town. McGilvray's statements regarding Tamil Muslims in Sri Lanka are summarized as follows:

> ...the frequency of Kuti [matri-clan] endogenous marriages is extremely low for the Moors [Muslims].... The social status of the opposite party's Kuti was never mentioned [in the marriage choices].... Individual statements about Kuti ranking...seemed hopelessly inconsistent and unreliable....The [Survey] data [also]...do not establish a clear set of ranked Kutis....[144]

Whatever the sociological reality of caste among Tamil Muslims, it was the belief of twenty new-Muslim respondents interviewed for this study that there is no caste among Muslims. Newspaper interviews with converts also confirm this belief. Perceptions may be more relevant in decision making than actual facts.

What are the bases of this perception? I think the common Indian is more likely to base a perception of social reality on observational knowledge than on any other source of information. What is most visible about Muslims for an untouchable is commensality and equality, not endogamy. Commensality among Tamil Muslims obscures whatever "casteness" the Muslim social subdivisions carry. Mines observes:

> All Muslim groups (subdivisions) and this applies to...the non-Tamil speaking subdivisions as well, interact socially on a basis of equality.... They all attend each other's celebrations and ceremonies and all readily eat together, sitting shoulder to shoulder.[145]

This commensality creates problems for social researchers. As one anthropologist noted about Tamil Muslims of Sri Lanka: "...observance of normal interaction did not promise to supply much data regarding whether any degree of consensus of...ranking existed among the Moors."[146] An untouchable is more likely to base perception on contrast and comparison, rather than using academic criteria. Such an individual is more likely to check whether the evils of the caste system are found or not found there in a community than to investigate whether the caste system itself exists. What is harmful are the ill effects of the caste system, even though at the same time one might be benefitting from one's own *jati's* ("sub caste") solidarity.[147] An untouchable dislikes the caste system because the individual is dealt with as an untouchable in the system. There is no commensality nor fellow feeling. Whereas a Hindu untouchable is not allowed to enter the temple, all Tamil Muslims can enter the mosque and pray shoulder to shoulder. Here there is no untouchable community to be seen. If untouchables do not find the evils of the caste system in the Muslim community, they are likely to conclude that there is no caste system in Islam.[148]

When an educated new Muslim was questioned about the lack of egalitarianism among Muslims by pointing out class differences between rich and poor, the young man's reply was, "But everyone prays together."

The evidence presented here suffices to conclude that the main features of caste: hierarchy, concept of pollution, lack of commensality, and endogamy, are not found among Tamil Muslims. The sources I have used here also establish that neither is the practice of occupational division found among Tamil Muslims. Therefore, the perception of untouchables in Tamil Nadu is based upon the fact that there are hardly any caste features among Muslims, but strongly visible egalitarian practices.

Political Strength of the Tamil Muslims

A study of Tamil Muslims' political support reveals that they adopted a regional strategy for their community interests which contrasts with an all-India Muslim trend supporting the Congress Party in the post-independent period. As early as 1954 and 1957, we find reports of Muslim support for the DMK.[149] For the 1962 election, the DMK formed an electoral alliance with the Muslim League.[150] This alliance continued for the next three elections. In 1967 and 1971 it worked against Congress and in 1980 against the ADMK, when it was allied with the Congress nationally. The Muslim League did not contest any election of the Legislative Council after the 1962 elections. Instead, its members contested as "independents." These Muslim "dummy candidates" were used to split votes by drawing support away from an opponent. Muslim support for the DMK not only appears in the shape of independents contesting the DMK's major opposition party, but also is accompanied by a general diversion of Muslim votes in the same direction. In interviews it became evident that Tamil Muslims are supporting both the parties, Muslim League and the DMK, and both the leaders, Abdus Samad and Karunanidhi, at the same time. This dual regional and communal color is expressed in the erstwhile Madras state by Muslims' cooperation with the Anti-Brahmin Movement, in the pre-independence pro-communal award campaign, and by Tamil Muslims' support to the Muslim League.[151] In their political responses, Tamil Muslims are similar to other Tamils in the sense of sharing in the regional politics of anti-Brahminism and Dravidian nationalism.

Unlike North Indian Muslims, Tamil Muslims did not suffer from the consequences of the communal conflict and its legacies. One can find a continuity in the different aspects of Tamil Muslim life: political, economic, and educational. The majority of Muslim elite in politics and business did not migrate to Pakistan, as those in North India did, leaving the followers without leadership. As a matter of fact, in the post-independence period, southern Muslim leaders such as Sait Ismail tried to fill the vacuum in the all-India Muslim leadership. This continuity in Tamil Nadu helped Muslims maintain their power and status, which must have affected the untouchables' perception of them.

The power position of the Tamil Muslims as compared to Muslims in North India is reflected in a sample survey conducted in a South Indian city, Tiruchirapalli, and in the North Indian city of Jabalpur. In response to the question, "How likely would you be to succeed if you tried to change a municipal regulation?" 58 percent of the Muslims in the South Indian city as compared to 12 percent of the Muslims in the North Indian city responded, "Very likely."[152] These responses reflect the confidence Tamil Muslim feel in comparison to the powerlessness of Muslims in North India.

Muslim Organizations in Tamil Nadu

An assessment of the Muslim organizations in Tamil Nadu and their missionary activities will be helpful in understanding their possible influence on the decision of untouchables to convert. There is no single Muslim "missionary network" in Tamil Nadu, in the sense of a Christian pattern of organization, complete with church, hospital, school, and other support institutions, which not only help poor untouchables as well as others but are also a material attraction towards Christianity.[153] A few Muslim organizations do preach Islam to non-Muslims and deal with the new Muslim affairs without such apparatus as Christians missionaries have. The South Indian Islamic Society and Jama'at-e-lslami Hind are the prominent ones.

The South Indian Islamic Society was established in 1940 by M.W. Abdur Rahman at Tirunelveli. Belying its name, the organization activities are limited to Tirunelveli where its office is situated. Its president, A.K. Rifaee, is a former member of the Tamil Nadu legislature. The organization does not publish any Islamic literature. It does not operate any hospital, school, or mosque. The organization does not even have any preacher or *maulavi* on its payroll. It was founded to help new converts who contact its office to recite *Kalima* and to send anyone who wants to know more about the new faith to any Islamic school. The Polyani school in Kerala had been such a place of education. The organization also provides an amount equivalent to four dollars for traveling expenses. In the time of its founder-president, the organization used to give a new outfit and a cap to each convert. Because it is a trust, its finances are legally subject to government audit.

Jama'at-e-Islami India was founded in 1941 by Sayyid Abul A'la Mawdudi (1903-1979). Mawdudi is considered to be the single most widely read scholar of the Muslim world today. Abul Lais Islahi is the current president of the Jama'at-e-Islami India with its headquarters at Delhi. Jama'at-e-Islami's objective is *Shahadat e Haq*. This Urduized Arabic term is a part of symbolic revivalist language. Literally, it means "being witness to truth." The organization's objective as written in its constitution is to convey the message of Islam to every citizen of India. Doctrinal position aside, Jama'at work is concentrated only among Muslims. The dominant features of its offices are libraries and reading rooms, drawing one to the conclusion that its work is largely concentrated among literate Muslims. Jama'at has translated its Urdu books on Islam and published them in various Indian languages. It has published translations of the Quran in fifteen languages. It publishes magazines and newspapers in almost all the significant languages of India. In Tamil Nadu, though Jama'at has a small presence, the availability of its books has been instrumental in presenting Islam to the educated non-Muslim Tamils. It has published about fifty-four books in Tamil.

Jama'at in Tamil Nadu is mainly a group of Urdu-speaking Muslims concentrated in northern Tamil Nadu and Madras, unlike the vast majority of Tamil Muslims who speak Tamil. Most of Jama'at literature has appeared in Tamil in the last decade. Its two-room state headquarters is more a publishing house than a party office. In one 10' x 12' room which has a name plate reading "Translation House," one can see a twenty-seven-year-old new Muslim busy translating the Quran from Hindi into Tamil. It is his kitchen and bedroom as well, which indicates the extent of finances available to him. The secretary of the Jama'at was confident that its literature has an impact on educated Tamils. He also said that Tamils are openminded, relatively unbiased, and willing to read Islamic literature. He thinks that this literature

7

The Environment of Decision

The Dravidian movement and its dynamics played an important role in mediating untouchables' aggressive behavior. The neo-Muslims' views shaped by the peculiar Tamil environment were part of the proximate cause in their conversions. The anti-Brahmin movement of the early twentieth century had located the source of the Tamil problems, especially of the historical discrimination against Adi-Dravadians (untouchables), in the Brahminic domination of the society. The most prominent contributors to this focus were Periyar E.V. Rama-swami Naicker's Justice party and the Dravida Kazhagam, established in 1944. Later on its message was carried on by a splinter group, the Dravida Munnetra Kazhagam (DMK, founded in 1949), under the leadership of Anna Durai, and in a milder way by its other factions and incarnations.

Anti-Brahminism and the Dravidian Movement

Dravidianism had its origin in the anti-Brahmin movement of the early twentieth century. It was a response to the continued Brahmin dominance in the power structure of Madras society.[154] This movement inspired the Justice party, which succeeded in mobilizing the interests of all the minority religious communities, non-Brahmin castes, and linguistic groups under a common ideology of communal equality based on a common dislike of Brahmin domination. Brahmin being Aryan and non-Brahmin being Dravidian provided a common cultural myth to the movement. The non-Brahmin elite drew from the South Indian cultural past that the Hindu caste system which gives Brahmins the highest position in caste hierarchy was unknown in the original Dravidian society.

Although the political power of the Justice party was short-lived, its anti-Brahmin ideology found new dynamism in the leadership of E.V. Ramaswami Naickar, founder of the "Self-respect Movement," which aimed to free India from Brahmin tyranny and the religion by which the Dravidian people were held in submission. He later organized the Dravidian Kazhagam, a radical and exclusively social movement. They persistently attacked the Brahminic versions of the Hindu texts. In 1945 they adopted a resolution calling for the establishment of a *Dravida Nadu*, a sovereign and casteless Dravidian nation in southern India. But since DMK's participation in the electoral process (from 1954), and subsequent control of the state government in 1967, the radicalism in their political agenda has been defused. However, Tamil Nadu still rejects northern Indian dominance by refusing to adopt Hindi, the national language of India, and regularly sides with the demand of greater autonomy to the state governments. What concerns us here is the socio-ideological component of the Dravidian movement, which was shared by all its organizational incarnations.

Anti-Hindu and Anti-Hindi Propaganda

The cultural agenda of the Dravidian movement had a much wider impact on Tamil society than its political program. Its opposition to Hindi has resulted in such a situation that it is difficult to find a single signpost written in Hindi in Tamil Nadu. In 1900, according to one estimate, half the words in the Tamil language had sanskritic influence; fifty years later, the influence of this "Aryan" language had been reduced to only a fifth.[155]

The early Dravidian movement was basically aimed at eliminating superstitious beliefs, customs, and untouchability on one hand and promoting rationalistic thinking on the other, but Hinduism bore the brunt of its criticism. "Superstition" and "exploitation" were the expressions frequently used by Periyar Ramaswami in his writings and speeches when describing the Hindu religion. Periyar's periodical *The Modern Rationalist* often contained articles denigrating and ridiculing Hindu concepts of God/gods. The titles themselves represent that attitude: "Divine Menstruation" (June 1972), "The God that Is a Devil" (September 1972), "Honeymoon in a Hindu Zoo" (March 1973), "Menstrual Pollution in Holy Temples" (June 1973), or "Obscenity Thy Name is Mahabharata" (November 1971).[156] Periyar publicly ridiculed the Hindu religious books as fairy tales, irrational and grossly immoral.

This anti-Hindu ideology was not limited to writings and speeches. Under Periyar's provocation, the Dravidian movement campaigned for the public burning of the *Manu* (sacred book of Hindu laws) and *Ramayana* (sacred mythology) on the grounds that they represented the northern/Aryan dominance over southern/Dravidian culture and were the basis of a totally inhuman caste system which gave Aryan Brahmins the dominant position in society. Besides public ceremonial burning of Hindu texts, the Dravidian movement regularly carried out campaigns in which temple idols were broken and untouchables were forcibly taken into temples in defiance of the Hindu prohibition against such entry. This attack on Hinduism was continued as late as 1971, when Periyar inaugurated a campaign of denigrating Hindu deities.

Impact of Dravidianism on Tamil Society and the Converts

This onslaught had a strong impact on political workers and educated people, if not so strong on the general masses. Barnett's survey notes the strongest impact on the DMK leadership itself: 74.3 percent of the local level DMK leaders said that they did not maintain traditional religious customs.[157] Although the masses had not left their religion, the same themes conveyed through film media—in a country where film actors are prominent politicians—focused on Hinduism as a source of the problem.[158] Adi-Dravidians, particularly, must have thought this way, being already at the bottom of the social pyramid. The denial of God, disobedience to the so-called priestly class (Brahmins) and criticism of holy books were no less revolutionary messages to these suppressed people. The movement's impact created a vacuum of belief. Renunciation of religion was no doubt a partial answer, but was it actually a solution? In the Indian atmosphere, mere renunciation of religion did not help.

Although Periyar and the Dravidian movement were referred to by the convert respondents in one way or another, only three were "Periyar-made" personalities. All three of these untouchables played leading roles in converting others. Rahmatullah (Margo Rajgopal) is a teacher and poet based in Matu Peth (in Thanjavur District) who has received two government prizes for being the best teacher. He proudly said that he participated in "Periyar's anti-Brahmin movement." Rahmatullah has converted 250 Adi-Dravidians to Islam. Ayyoob Khan, brother of the leader of conversion in Kurayoor, said that he also participated in one of the Periyar's radical activities. Accompanied by his friends, he forcibly entered a big temple in Madurai shouting to the priest, "We are Hindu, let us enter." Another leader, Abdul Hadi, recalled joining the blackshirt movement of Periyar. Even for marriage he chose a time which fell during Rahukalam (an inauspicious period for Hindu marriage). He said, "My association with the Periyar movement for a long time taught me hatred against the oppressive caste system of Hindu society."

Tamil people in general may be more accommodating to other religious communities than North Indians.[159] I have already discussed the "Tamilness" of Muslims in Tamil Nadu, which seems to be one of the sources of harmony there. Periyar's image of Muslims is also very positive:

> The Muslims in South India are all Dravidians. Historians and research scholars are of the same view. Even the Muslims accept it unhesitantly. In the matter of habit, classification, divisions and differences, there is a striking contrast between the Aryans and Dravidans. At the same time there are not even a hundred odd differences between a Tamilian and a Muslim.[160]

Racial/cultural reasons aside, the political scenario itself was enough to avoid northern-style communal polarization in Tamil Nadu. Not only were Muslim economic interests the same as those of other backward classes in the anti-Brahmin movement, but Muslims' dislike of Brahmins corresponded with the Dravidian hostility to "Aryan" Brahmins. Periyar also gave full support to the scheme for Pakistan.[161] Tamil Muslim antagonism to the Congress party is in part responsible for their long soldarity with DMK. The dynamics of Dravidian ideology and politics as a third force prevented Tamil politics from becoming polarized on a communal basis. This lack of communal polarization helped Muslims retain their position. Parallel to the religious idioms and symbolism of the nationalist movement in the rest of India, here was an anti-Aryan ideology which, instead of having communal overtones, had a soft corner for other religious communities. Periyar and Anna Durai, leaders of the Tamil nationalist movement, had diametrically opposite personalities, ideology and politics to those of Tilak, Aurobindo, and Lajpat Rai, whose revivalist politics and influence, mainly in the north, had the inevitable consequence of communal polarization in North India.

There are several manifestations of better communication with Muslims in Tamil society. For instance, books on Islam are more readily available in Madras than in Delhi, as evidenced by annual book fairs in each place. Newspapers in Tamil Nadu frequently carry articles on Islam which Muslims find to be quite objective analyses, whereas in North India, Muslims perceive the media to be hostile. This difference is typified by media *Eid* reports: Bombay and Madras newspapers carried articles on the celebrations, whereas in Delhi and Calcutta (where more Muslims live), newspapers had no items on this primary socio-religious event of India's largest minority (see Table 7).

The above argument does not mean that Muslims do not have a negative identity in Tamil Nadu. They do, though with comparative less hatred and tension. There was an average of four riots per year in Tamil Nadu between 1954 and 1968, while the average for the same years in UP was seventeen and the national average 199 per year.[162] Communal violence remained concentrated in the north. But reporting of these incidents in the south nevertheless has contributed to the negative image of Muslims. The derogatory word for Muslim in Tamil is still *Turukudu*, derived from "Turk," conveying an image of foreigner and invader,[163] despite the fact that the Dravidian origin of Tamil Muslims is historically established.

Blending of Dravidian Ideals and the Islamic Concept of Tawhid

Tawhid in its literal sense is "a relationship with the Only One that excludes a similar relationship with any one else." *Tawhid* is the single

most important belief, term, and concept in Islam. Islamic scholars
have used this term to describe the whole Islamic way of life. Discussing the implication of this belief on human relations, one Indian scholar
summarizes *Tawhid* as follows:

> In the human context it means emancipation and restoration of man's
> essential freedom from all human and (man-made) super-human bon-
> dages before his commitment to Allah can be genuine and positive. Man
> is free. He is bound to no other man, group of men, or to their mores
> and manners, customs and traditions, social institutions, laws, modes of
> thought, views and presumptions, theories and philosophies. Man is
> under no obligation to submit to any authority or commit to anyone's
> will. He owes nothing to any being other than Allah, to whom he owes
> everything, even his own existence.[164]

This explanation of *Tawhid* makes it a statement in "liberation theology," within an Indian context. But this concept is not a contemporary reconstruction. "Emancipation of men from submission to human
beings" is considered by Muslims the task of prophets.[165]

The Quran, presenting its model of intergroup relations for the
ummah declares: "O Mankind, we have created you all out of one pair,
a male and a female. We have constituted you into peoples and tribes
that you may know one another. Noblest among you in the eyes of
God is the most righteous."[166] This and other verses on a similar
theme are among the oft-used verses of Quran in *juma Khutbas* ("Friday
sermons"). Similar is the usage of the prophet Muhammad's procla-
mation at his farewell pilgrimage to Mecca: "All men issue from Adam
and Adam issued from dust. Therefore, no Arab may claim distinction
over a non-Arab except in piety and righteousness."[167]

Throughout Muslim history these ideals have exerted great influence on the Muslim community. In the situation under study, it is
possible that untouchables somehow came across these concepts by
their interaction with Muslims, as suggested in the last chapter. Or
they became aware of these themes in the contemporary Islamic literature available in Tamil. It is also possible that they formulated this
notion of "One God One Creed" as a convenient ideological explanation for their conversion. "Ideas and values may be used to rationalize
deeds once done."

The anti-Hindu rebellious idioms and the ideals of casteless society in
contrast to the Islamic belief of *Tawhid* in the perception of Tamil Adi-
Dravidians (untouchables) resulted in an interesting formulation which
may have attracted these untouchables to Islam. The interpretation of the

concept of oneness of God for the purpose of egalitarian ideology had been previously almost unheard of. In Abdul Hadi's words, "one God one Creed" is the "most solid foundation for equality." Implicit is the contrast with the many gods and castes of Hinduism. An old activist even recalled Periyar as saying, "There can be no objection to a God that endeavours to make the high and low in the society live as equals."

It seems that the new Muslims quoted above were consciously or unconsciously blending the themes of the Dravidian movement with the belief of *tawhid* in Islam. The Dravidian slogan "One God One Caste"[168] was conveniently amended by those new Muslims to read "One Creed" instead of "One Caste."

In any case, this embedding of Dravidian ideals of a casteless society and the Islamic concept of *tawhid* in the minds of converts indicates the uniqueness of the Tamil matrix. It is therefore safe to conclude that the option for Islam is facilitated by Dravidian ideology and by the lack of communal hatred and tension in the environment of decision-making in Tamil Nadu,[169] whereas the egalitarian ideals of Islam have served as an attraction or a justifying ideology in retrospect.

8

Why Conversion?

Why Didn't Converts Opt
for Physical Violence?

An answer to this question could be searched out by asking what options untouchables have in India today: (1) To pursue their rights within the system in a legal framework, including politics; (2) to join an anti-system ideology of change such as Marxism; (3) to fight injustice in a Naxalite way, i.e., violent rebellion.

I have already discussed the frustration of the untouchables with the first option. The political strength of the dominant castes, their manipulation of administrative apparatus, overall institutional decay, and the deterioration of law and order in India, are prominent points of frustration with political and legal options, whereas the nature of the untouchable problem is value-oriented. It is rooted in the society, and the legislative constitutional option has its limitation in this sphere. Nevertheless, as compared to the other options, this one is being pursued with patience by the largest number of untouchables. In a given situation this option is better than suffering injustice, though it is more or less a part of the status quo and is not considered a strategy of change by the more militant anti-system stratum of untouchables.

As far as the second option is concerned, it is almost non-revolutionary because of the dynamics of democracy and caste in India. "In Tanjore [Thanjavur] the communists made a major effort to organize the Harijan workers, taking up caste issues and even organizing them on the basis of existing caste assemblies. But this very success made the communists in Tanjore a Party of Pallars and Paraiyans [untouchable castes]." A frustrated leader of the Communist Party of India-Marxist (CPI-M) rightly asked: "Where do I go from here? Am I making a Harijan revolution?"[170]

Although the leader's dream of revolution is frustrated, his party has absorbed a number of revolutionary untouchables. At the local level it also has eased the life of untouchables by organizing some of them, an achievement underestimated by a revolutionary zealot. The commissioner's survey data on untouchability in Thanjavur[171] shows this distinction with the lowest level of untouchability offenses (see note 32). It is a credit to this Marxist mobilization of untouchables. In search of a way to revolution, however, since 1977 the CPI-M has again revised its tactical line as regards the peasantry, reverting back to its pre-1967 "middle peasant" line.[172] At present the party leaders show great reluctance to take any action in favor of the rural poor that they feel is likely to antagonize the middle peasants.[173] This reversion of strategy clearly shows the limits of this option for untouchables as a whole.

At some places in Tamil Nadu, educated untouchable youths called Naxalite did turn to violent methods for self help and quick justice. Although no one in Tamil Nadu is working under the name of Naxalite, the government is using the label as an easy license for its repressive activities. The police reaction is wider and harsher than the violence of these so-called Naxalites. In 1980, police action began in Dharmapuri District on August 6, when a bomb went off in a police car. In the year following that incident, government clearly demonstrated that its coercive capability is far greater than the tiny bomb blast which killed none. Police action included 15,000 new recruits to the police force, three new police stations, and a force of 2,000 specially armed policemen. Police also sponsored anti-Naxalite committees composed of local landlords.[174] An extra deputy superintendent of police and additional inspectors were appointed. An anti-Naxalite cell was formed and rewards of Rs.10,000 for any information about Naxalites was announced. In one year many mass rallies of the untouchables were interrupted, hundreds were arrested and tortured in illegal custody, at least nineteen were killed—including the charismatic organizer, 29-year-old Balan, a M.Sc. dropout who mobilized large masses of people in at least four talukas of Dharmapuri District within two years.[175] This was almost an end to this episode of "Naxalite" activity. Young militant untouchables here were crushed before they could satisfy even some of their revolutionary passion.

As discussed in an earlier chapter, Naxalites are the only group that uses violence as a strategy. All other clashes or violent conflicts are more isolated assertions and reactions to violence than a part of any strategy of change. This Naxalite pattern involves mobilization, and surfaces only at certain spots. Those outside that region can sympathize, but cannot participate unless they are mobilized in their area by an extraordinarily active militant ideology. Moreover, the very imbalance created by the state's coercive power and the possibility of harsh consequences teaches a lesson of restraint to less militant but equally frustrated individuals, especially those who are a bit better off than the agricultural laborers organized by the late Mr. Balan.

There may be many reasons that the response of the untouchables is not so violent or so widespread as it could be. One might be that "[t]raditional Indian ideas of conflict management. . . tend to de-emphasize. . . overt clashes."[176] A majority of untouchables still cannot afford to be violent. From the utilitarian point of view, the cost/risk balance of Naxalite-type activity is also quite uninspiring. Although this revolutionary method promises a long-term change for the community, it does limit the short term chances of social mobility (economic benefits and security of property and life). A substantial number of the untouchable elite, whom we have considered as frustrated, sensitive, but economically better off, probably do not want to risk their achieved status for an evidently unviable revolutionary strategy.

This is the situation in which some militant individuals have turned towards a non-violent but hurtful, legal but anti-system, active and provocative strategy of protest: conversion. This option has always been in the air for oppressed people in Tamil Nadu. Tamil Nadu has a contemporary tradition of conversion to Christianity and Islam. A few neo-Muslims mentioned in the interviews that they had been thinking of conversion since the 1940s. One convert (Rahmat) had stopped worshiping Hindu deities in 1946 as a result of his study of Islam's prohibition of idol worship. Abdul Hadi said, "Since I was a child my father wanted to make me a Muslim and that is why he did not allow my ears to be pierced, as Muslims do not do it to boys."

Because of the relative powerlessness of untouchables against clearly identifiable oppressors, conversion, like Gandhi's *satyagraha* or Martin Luther King's nonviolent resistance, provides a technique for the manifestation of discontent. Conversion comes close to the Rudolphs' explanation of Gandhi's nonviolence as the strategy of those without material means of resistance. Gandhian *satyagraha* and conversion are both non-violent; both actions are rooted in tradition and are fired by the passions of liberty and dignity. The Gandhian one is non-constitutional while this one is anti-system. Both the non-violent militancies have occasionally inspired violent reactions from the side they are directed against. Gandhi challenged the legitimacy of the colonial regime; conversion challenges the legitimacy of the dominant value system. The *satyagraha* method of action was suited to the "non-fighting twice-born castes. . . who provided the core of nationalist leadership."[177] Likewise, conversion-type protest is in accord with the traditionally compliant non-fighting outcastes. The only difference—an important one—is that conversion comes under the category of "hurting without shedding blood," whereas *satyagraha* was aimed, philosophically at least, at eliciting "the better element" in an oppressor.

This answer to "Why conversion? Why not physical aggression?" is a general explanation. A person's behavior may have its exclusive reasons. People in the same situation do behave differently. A social scientist may look for socio-economic reasons, or search for the factors influencing decision makers' perceptions, to give a proximate cause of why people follow this tactic rather than that tactic, but the exact cause of a decision could be as individualistic as possible. It is human beings we are dealing with!

Why Not Christianity?

There are more Christians than Muslims in Tamil Nadu. Almost all of them are converts of the last two centuries. They have a functioning network of educational and social welfare institutions, while Muslims have no welfare scheme of their own and fewer colleges to serve their community needs. Christian missionaries' educational contribution is evident in the higher percentage of literacy in the southern districts where they are concentrated. If the option of conversion is so well known in Tamil Nadu, it is due to the exemplar of Christian conversion. Keeping these facts in mind, our question becomes important, for not only did the untouchables under study not convert to Christianity, but, ironically, some Christian ex-untouchables also converted to Islam.

The first point of answer is related to the Christian tradition of conversion in India itself. Christianity in India was preached by foreign priests under the colonial umbrella in the past two centuries. Taking note of this reality, Kananaikil comments that "the [Christian] conversion movement was...still a response to outside forces, and relied largely on outside leadership and inspiration."[178] After independence, the former advantage of conversion to the religion of the ruler became a disadvantage, if not a stigma.[179]

In the early phase of the missionaries' work, caste was considered a social system, not an evil as it appeared to them later. Therefore, it became a considered strategy to work, convert, and establish churches on caste lines. This adaptation or "indigenization" even resulted in the production of a fifth Veda ("Christian Veda"). The famous Italian Jesuit, Roberto Nobili, used to call himself a "Roman Brahmin."[180] Consequently this missionary strategy became a handicap for later Jesuits who seriously fought against this social evil. The wall dividing churches on caste lines remained into the twentieth century.[181] This historical mistake, although a result of the overadaptation to social reality, not a doctrinal problem, is still alive in the shape of Christian "castes" in Tamil Nadu. One regularly hears and reads of Nadar Christians, Fernandu Christians, Scheduled Caste Christians, and such caste names.[182] These untouchable Christians are largely as helpless as non-Christian untouchables. Their socio-economic situations are almost the same. There have even been riots between "touchable" and untouchable Christians.[183] Commensality could not be established among different caste levels of Christian converts. This prevalence of caste in Christianity has been the only reason for conversion given by new Muslims of Christian origin in the press.[184]

The dependence of untouchables on the educational and welfare network of the missionaries has also declined because other means have become available. These charities no longer create the soft corner necessary for "encapsulation," since these things have become a part of public life. Furthermore, as this study suggests, conversion in Tamil Nadu is no longer an act only of poor and illiterate people, who could be attracted through hospitals, schools, and the like. These people are educated and economically mobile. For them status, equality, and power are more relevant, sought-after objectives.

Conversion to Christianity in Tamil Nadu does not satisfy untouchables' demand for equal treatment. It also does not come close to the protest requirement of these converts, as Christianity has a less negative identity in India since the departure of the British. The option of Christianity could not have made the conversion as vocal and spectacular an exit as it is now. Islam and Muslims have the highest, most challenging negative identity in India, sought by the "little Ambedkars" for protest purposes.

Observing trends in Indian Christianity, one anthropologist reports that the process of retroversion and indigenization is expected to be intensified in the future.[185] If the process of the "indigenization" of Christianity is not checked by some sort of liberation theology, Christianity in India might gradually lose its identity and become another Buddhism. This might be good for the Christians' prospects of socioeconomic mobility in India, but bad for future proselytizing.

Need for a dependable ally was another necessity of these converts. The untouchables of Meenakshipuram opted to fight for their rights, but their two years' experience, preceding the conversion, discussed in detail in the Meenakshipuram Report, clearly suggested that to fight the dominant caste and the local administration it manipulated, they needed more strength and power. They joined the Muslim community— or sought an ally. Subsequent events suggest that it did work. Christians in Tamil Nadu have neither the political clout of caste Hindus nor the community solidarity of Muslims, nor have they the militant image of Muslims. "Khan"—connoting, in South Asia, strength and power— is the preferred part of the Muslim name among these converts. Physical protection is a need for these sensitive and assertive untouchables. In the increasingly violent Indian society, self-help is becoming a major strategy for many non-dominant communities. A political alliance helps the numerically small groups. Communities have a tradition of these alliances in the region. In 1933 Ezhavas (an untouchable jati), Christians, and Muslims of Kerala had such an alliance.[186] In Tirunelvely District of Tamil Nadu, in the major anti-untouchable riots of 1899, Nadars sought Muslims' protection against Thevars when the government apparatus failed. Hundreds of them even became Muslims.[187]

Why Not Buddhism?

The neo-Buddhist movement led by Dr. Ambedkar was the first mass conversion of the "liberated untouchables" of independent India. It was a demonstration of untouchable will, not a result of missionary persuasion under the imperial umbrella. Why did the converts under study not follow the path of their charismatic leader, Ambedkar?

Although neo-Buddhism was a self-chosen path, the mass conversion was largely on caste lines. It was a Mahar movement. Very few untouchables converted to Buddhism in Tamil Nadu. Therefore, this option was not as well-known a choice in Tamil Nadu as conversion to Christianity. Secondly, Buddhism, for all practical purposes, had died out in India by the tenth century of the Common Era. The whole image of Buddhism in India today is nothing but the achievement and experience of the neo-converts themselves. Unlike the Christian, Sikh, and Muslim minorities of India which convey certain images of identity, status, and power, Buddhism prior to the neo-Buddhists had no adjectives ordinarily applied to it. Therefore, conversion to Buddhism could not become a strategy of social mobility.

The term *neo-Buddhist* has become more or less synonymous with the terms *untouchable* or *Harijan*. Neo-Buddhists could not get rid of the old identity and its problems by merging themselves into a new identity, as there did not exist an independent identity of Buddhism before them. There was no known pattern of Buddhists relationship with other communities at the grass roots level of human interaction which could help untouchables change their position vis-à-vis Hindus. Therefore, they are still being treated by dominant castes as they were before. The Maharashtra riots of 1978 and a constant high rate of atrocities against them established the fact that the same stigmas are attached to this "changed" identity as well. The problems, issues, and movements of the neo-Buddhists are similar to those of other untouchables. For the stratum of untouchables which we are discussing, Buddhism is not a live option, as some of my respondents said. Professor Trevor Ling, an authority on Buddhism, concluded a recent study by saying, "Whatever movement or ideology captures the allegiance of the majority of untouchables, it is unlikely now to be neo-Buddhism."[188]

Amazingly, conversion to Buddhism is seen as such a mild action that it is commended even by RSS (Rashtriya Swayamsevak Sangh, a Hindu chauvinist organization violently opposed to conversions).[189] Like Christianity, Buddhism does not have the kind of challenging negative identity which can manifest the protest nature of the decision commensurate with the intensity of discontent found among untouchables today. Neo-Buddhism is no more a promising identity, much less a powerful ally or a strategy for social status. (See the note on Dr. Ambedkar's conversion in Appendix II.)

9

Arab Connection and Inducement

The national debate following the conversion news focused on "the Arab connection" as the single most important factor. This charge of the use of money as an inducement to convert was first published by the *Organiser*, a newsweekly of Hindu revivalism.[190] Later, it appeared more or less in every paper and in statements of public leaders. Even the late prime minister, Mrs. Gandhi, told *The New York Times* that "enormous amounts of Arab money are coming in. And they have made a conscious effort to convert the very poor, mostly harijans, and in one place, some Christians as well."[191] Although the charge of using cash inducement (Rs 500, i.e. $45, per head) for conversion is the most common factor repeatedly discussed in the press, the offer of a job in the Persian Gulf and the impact of revivalist tendencies among Muslims are also occasionally mentioned.

As far as possibilities are concerned, all of these three factors are feasible propositions. One of the heads of expenditure for *zakat*[192] is *Taleef-al-Koloob*, financial help to a new Muslim.[193] It is a tradition in some parts of South Asia that new Muslims are honored by the community, by having presented to them one or two sets of clothing, a neighborhood feast, sweets, and some money. As far as the availability of Arab money is concerned, this is also not an impossible supposition. Whether it is a Miami mayor who stood at the door of Prince Alfassi in

1982 to get a donation for a stadium, or the late Mrs. Gandhi who received a Rs.200 million donation for the Asian Games from the Sheikh of Kuwait, "no one is refused at the door of a Sheikh." It is quite possible that someone might have acquired some money for this "Islamic cause." As for smuggling this amount into India, it is also said to be an easy thing in a country where the underground economy is sometimes estimated at 40 percent of the size of the legitimate economy—and even that might be an understatement.[194] A long coast and lightly checked borders with Nepal and Sri Lanka plus the practice of the *hundy* system (illegal and extralegal money transactions) from Indian overseas workers in the Gulf and Southeast Asian countries makes it possible to get money—not to mention people and goods—in or out of India.[195]

This situation both makes any inquiry into foreign money difficult to investigate, and an allegation of the same easier to fabricate. For that reason, charges of foreign financing have currency in India. Mrs. Gandhi alleged that there were foreign hands and money in the Assam massacres of 1983, in the Sikh crisis of Punjab in 1984, and in other incidents of this sort. As far as the *Meenakshipuram Report* is concerned, the investigator reports that the caste Hindus who alleged such foreign hands could not furnish "any detail as to who paid to whom, etc." The report concludes, after confidential inquiries with some of the non-converted untouchables: "It is not possible to say in this regard anything categorically about the involvement of the foreign money."[196]

Every one of the new Muslim respondents interviewed for this study categorically denied the charge and one furiously asked, "Why don't they purchase us back to Hinduism if we are on sale?" Two of the new converts said that instead of getting money, they spent some for conversion. Muhammad Qasim of Karuppiah said, "We asked a Muslim who resides next door to make us Muslims, but he did not help. So we went to a neighboring village and spent Rs. 300 and wasted a week to bring a *maulavi* who could help us recite *Kalima*." A government servant at Madurai said that he would commit suicide if it were proved that he had been bought. This charge so commonly believed in the press infuriates converts and non-convert untouchables alike because it questions the very dignity untouchables are looking for.

The fact is that money is of little attraction to these converts, who are relatively better off economically. It is also important to note that Muslims, even prosperous Tamil Muslims, can hardly offer inducements to match the government concessions that untouchables are foregoing by being converted. One new Muslim from Kurayoor responded to the question of "500 Rupees for conversion" that he has irrigated land; he takes two crops and the price of one of his she-buffalos is Rs. 2,000; why should he go for Rs. 500? Another one, with aspirations to leadership, asked, "If monetary incentive is the motive, why did not other equally poor or poorer Thevars [who are caste Hindus] embrace Islam for Arab money or a job in the Middle East?" It is not the material benefits, it is their self-respect the decision involves.

As for the charm of a Gulf job, no reporters, including those of the communal press, have yet reported any convert's leaving for a Gulf job. There are several reasons why this "Gulf job" hypothesis is not likely to explain conversions. Overseas jobs are not a new option for southern India. Over one-third of the unskilled workers exported to Malaysia by the British were untouchables.[197] There is an old tradition of finding overseas work in Southeast Asia as well as in the Gulf, which has tended more towards the Gulf since the sixties. Tamil Muslims and Malabaries (from Kerala) have been commercially connected with the Gulf for centuries and were the first to avail themselves of the opportunities offered by the oil companies. Out of four million Indians who live abroad, a half million reside in the Middle East.[198] (The 6.6 million Indians who have foreign citizenship are not included in these statistics.) Anyone who has visited the Gulf knows that the migrant community there is a kind of mini-India; Hindus, Muslims, and Christians all are found there. Therefore, neither is the charm of the Gulf peculiarly associated with Muslims only, as is assumed in the "Gulf job" hypothesis, nor is it as new an opportunity for southern peoples as it looks to an analyst from North India.

Availability of Islamic literature in Tamil could be said to be related to the phenomenon of Islamic revival, and perhaps is a result of foreign money. But this literature consists of translations of Urdu or Hindi, not Arabic, works. The authors are all Indians and the publishers are actually Tamil. I would say that Indian Muslims themselves have enough Islamic interests of their own to spend their money for an Islamic cause such as translating Islamic literature. Considering the size of the Indian market, the publication of some books in Tamil is not difficult to understand. There is at best an indirect relationship between a literature and conversion, as is suggested by the millions of copies of the hundreds of titles of foreign-printed communist ideological literature. Leaving the issue of the Gulf involvement aside, the growing number of Islamic publications is a part of revivalist tendencies among Muslims.

In the absence of any evidence for "Gulf money," the question becomes more significant: Why then this charge, so much believed, repeated, and even mentioned by a prime minister? It seems that the charge was based on the misperception that these converted untouchables are poor. This factor, in conjunction with another misperception—that Tamil Muslims are also poor—probably leads to the conclusion that Arabs are paying poor Muslims to convert poor untouchables.[199] This is the reason press reporters, political leaders, and public officials all demanded a better economic deal and an improved implementation of economic programs for untouchables. This attitude also helped many untouchables in all parts of the country to gain office-holders' ears by threats of conversion. But, as I have discussed in detail, these converts are not in bad shape economically. Northern reports also asked how these poor Muslims could afford to give money to untouchables. This question is correct in relation to the general economic situation of northern Muslims, but it is a misperception as regards Tamil Muslims. Interestingly, Muslims in the north also had this misperception. They sent truckloads of used clothing and shoes for these supposedly "needy" new Muslim fellows.

"A common misperception...to see the behavior of others as more centralized, planned, and coordinated than it is" has also given credence to this myth of Arab connection. If the Muslim press in the Middle East looks for a Zionist conspiracy behind each important negative development in world politics, the Indian press can similarly connect events like this to the money which was once allegedly used in an attempt to buy an atomic bomb. (Libyan Col. Gaddafi, according to press reports, tried to buy one from China.) Although these are stereotyped images and should not be taken seriously, such stereotypes do have influence. The popular acceptance of this theory is also due to its compatibility with a well-known standard pattern of explanation in India and many other Third World countries that the CIA, KGB and their "monies" are always at work. This theory, therefore, results from the "masking effect" of the pre-existing beliefs.

Pressure on media and government to reach a quick conclusion about this unique occurrence on such a touchy issue as conversion might have also resulted in their offering this hypothesis. In the later reports, some of the press itself began taking note of the better economic position of these untouchables and the relatively higher socio-economic status of Tamil Muslims.

The continued mistrust between Hindu and Muslim communities has also given currency to this hypothesis. Indian history textbooks negatively depict the medieval period of Indian history, popularly considered a Muslim period.[200] The recent memory of bitter fights between the two communities on the Pakistan issue and an increasing occurrence of communal riots in India proper does not even need a history lesson. These images of conflicting communities, for some, shape the interpretation of incoming information. In this atmosphere, it is quite easy for communalist mobilizers to connect the conversion and about one percent decrease in ten years in the proportion of Hindus in Tamil Nadu, into a Muslim conspiracy and in turn call for Hindu revivalism. Otherwise, rationally speaking, "the notion that some people somewhere really can manipulate social events, can plan, direct and control the outcome of complicated social relationships, is naive."[201]

10

Epiphenomenon: Hindu Revivalism

It appears that in most cases of aggressive behavior it is not only the form and intensity of manifestation but the outcome as well that determines and confers the title of that action. "Revolution" is merely turmoil, civil strife and lawlessness, unless it is successful. That is why there is no "abortive revolution" found in history. Likewise "freedom fighters" are seen as terrorists and rebels if they fail. This may be what inspired Nieburg to observe that "social change often pursues a logic that defies prediction and is logical only in retrospect."[202] This conversion could also be called the eccentric action of a few instead of a protest, if the whole non-eccentric population had not reacted so disproportionately.

The reaction started with the *Indian Express* on April 12, 1981, headline, "A whole village goes Islamic" (although the southern press was publishing the same kind of news for at least three months). The national press turned the relevant rural areas of southern Tamil Nadu into a pilgrimage center for journalists. Hardly a publication of national or local standing missed a special story on conversion, to say nothing of the hundreds of small news items, statements, demands, and coverage of rallies condemning conversion. Presidents of political parties, religious leaders and workers, ministers and government officials all paid visits to the "affected areas." Although this frantic reaction to conversion has gradually waned, the Hindu revivalist mobilization still continues, contributing to the rise of Hindu "cultural nationalism."

The whole reaction could be defined in three overlapping phases: first, the immediate reactions of Hindus; second, wave of untouchables' threats to convert, mainly in the North; and last, the Hindu revivalist mobilization and communal tension which resulted in the escalation of riots.

A Shock to the Majority Community

The immediate reaction was one of shock, even panic. "It was argued that the conversions were an attempt to destabilize the region and carried within them a potential of destroying the freedom and integrity of the country."[203] An important aspect of the orthodox Hindu reaction was a fear that conversions could affect the numerically dominant position of the Hindus in India. They painted a bleak future for Hinduism based on some statistical projection that Hindus will become a minority in India by the year 2281. Other computations concluded that Tamil Nadu will become a Muslim majority state in 2231.[204] Conversion was believed to be an assault on Hindus and Hinduism by Muslims. Inflammatory statements, such as the implausible threat of their becoming a minority, used by the Hindu revivalist organizations, gave birth to a deep sense of vulnerability among Hindus, which created extremely defensive reactions throughout India.[205] Two of the most important features of the Hindu reaction were a show of anger toward the Muslim community and a universal belief on the involvement of the petro-dollars. Hindu organizations in general demanded that conversions from Hinduism to other religions should be banned.

Threats of Conversion

Since this conversion of a few thousand to Islam was perceived as a threat to Hinduism and to India, it created a reaction which had no resemblance to the "murmurs and mild expressions of anger" heard when Dr. Ambedkar, along with approximately four million untouchables embraced Buddhism in 1956.[206] This Hindu response demonstrated to the leaders of the untouchables that their protest did work and that "the Muslims were the only minority in the country that Hindus took seriously." It provided an opportunity for the untouchables "to use the threat of conversion as a weapon against the Hindu backlash and to impress upon the Hindu community at large that the problem of their uplift was very much still there to be resolved."[207] This "vocal exit" inspired certain recuperative steps. Religious and political leaders of all kinds called for a relaxation of caste rules and removal of untouchability. Propaganda against preferential policies favoring untouchables was stopped. Even at New Delhi's Birla Mandir, a hundred chosen untouchables were anointed by the head priest at a Janmashtami prayer meeting,[208] a concession which Hindu opinion would otherwise have been most reluctant to grant. All these responses meant that the reaction to protest-conversion itself confirmed the success of the tactic, and suggested a further use of it. This was the second phase of conversion, when almost every day there were announcements from different untouchable individuals and groups that they would convert on such-and-such a date if their demands were not met. Newspapers rightfully characterized these statements as "threats" of conversion.

Violence and the Revivalist Mobilization of the Hindu Majority

The third phase of reaction was revivalist mobilization to "save Hinduism." It was accompanied by counter-conversion and reconversions to Hinduism in different parts of India, especially in the North. This period created communal tensions and resulted in riotings. The revivalist mobilization gained momentum in an all-India rally called Virat Hindu Sammelan, held on October 18, 1981 in Delhi and attended by 800,000 persons "mostly. . . middle class."[209] A confederation of all major Hindu organizations, named Vishva Hindu Parishad, formed branches all over India and has become the major revivalist group in India today. An untouchable leader who was present at the rally summarized the focus of this period: "There was hardly any reference to atrocities and other crimes like violation of human rights, exploitation and economic miseries at the Sammelan. The untouchables' leader commented that 'they want to save us from Islam, not atrocities.' ''[210] By this time, the low-key rhetoric of reform had given way to an all-out call for Hindu revivalism.

Parishad, RSS, and all other national and local organizations were vocal in their anger. They made it clear that "Mass conversion and communal peace can not live together."[211] Even the national press carried articles and editorials to that effect.[212] They were serious. Revivalist mobilization of Hindus by massive rallies, religious performances and *yatras* ("pilgrimages") throughout India resulted in a series of communal clashes, first in the erstwhile peaceful Tamil Nadu, and later on throughout India. These riots involved Hindu revivalists on one side and Christian, Muslims, or untouchables on the other side. The first clashes in Tamil Nadu took place in Kanyakumari, on March 1, 1982. Their targets were Christians who resisted the offensive revivalist propaganda and activity by outsiders in their localities.

Since Tamil Nadu is used to communal harmony, it took sixteen months of revivalist mobilization after the Meenakshipuram conversions to create such a tension in the relevant areas. The first major Hindu-Muslim riot in Tamil Nadu took place in June 1982 in Puliangudi. But these riots still had some features peculiar to the region: Muslims and untouchables (non-converts) were jointly confronting the dominant Thevar caste.[213] In 1981 there were seventeen, and in 1982 twenty, communal riots in Tamil Nadu, as compared to an average of 4 per year earlier.

In India as a whole, the number of riots rose from 319 in 1981 to 474 in 1982.[214] Similarly, the number of untouchables murdered in India rose from 571 in 1981 to 837 in 1983.[215] The number of administrative districts affected by communal violence grew from 216 in 1979 to 250 out of a total of 399.[216] Mourning the climate of violence, *India Today* observed: ''. . . ordinary Hindus—perfectly reasonable, even kindly folks—applaud sectarian violence because 'it is time we taught them a lesson.' ''[217]

The Reconversion Movement

Hindu revivalist technique also involved reconversion efforts targeted at Christians and Muslims. The Parishad began a massive nationwide campaign to "restore" Indian Muslims to the Hindu fold. This *Shuddhi* ("purification," meaning reconversion) effort had already achieved some success in Rajasthan State, where a few thousand Muslims were converted to Hinduism (a few thousand, according to Hindu organizations and national media, but a few hundred as admitted by Muslims).[218] Throughout 1982 there were numerous news items in the press about Christians "embracing" Hinduism.[219] There were several contested claims of the revivalist organizations about the reconversion of new Muslims as well. These reconversion stories helped raise the sagging morale of the Hindu majority after Meenakshipuram. Now Parishad's ten-year plan is "aimed at thwarting the plans of Christian and Muslim organizations to lure untouchables into their fold with the aid of foreign money." It plans to station one or two Hindu missionaries in each district of India. Private businesses, including such conglomerates as Birlas, are said to be contributing in their plans.[220]

The wave of Hindu revivalist reaction to conversions, which became a national movement, is sustained by the events in Punjab (1984-) involving the Sikh community and a successful movement for the reclamation of the Babri Mosque to Hindus (1983-86).[221] It is mainly due to the Hindu revivalist mobilization that, in the eighties, "Hinduism began to become a condition of national consciousness."[222]

The Official Response of the National Leadership

The Hindu revivalists were able to shape responses of the national leadership through their mass mobilization. Revivalist issues, it seemed for a while, became the national agenda. Fifty-seven percent of Indians polled wanted government intervention to stop conversions. The support was as high as 78 percent in the northern Indian cities.[223] This support, combined with the realization that religious chauvinist organizations which numbered less than a dozen in 1951, according to a government estimate, have now grown to over 500 with an active membership that runs into several millions,[224] started influencing those who care for people's votes—the politicians.

Politicians in power, always mindful of their popularity graphs, seeing the revivalist current, adopted its propaganda as their agenda. Prime minister Indira Gandhi and Home Minister (later President of India) Zail Singh took the lead in developing an official response to the conversions. The Prime Minister sided with the Hindu revivalist rhetoric when she bought the hypothesis of "Gulf Money" and implied that the converted untouchables were not acting on their own. In a press conference she observed that "what is obviously objectionable is if people's poverty and hardships are exploited for conversion."[225] She, obviously taking sides with majority sentiment, blamed the Muslim community for trying to convert untouchables with the help of Arab monetary support.[226] The Prime Minister's reaction to conversion was so similar to the revivalists' stand that it was officially praised by the RSS ("Rashtriya Swayamsevak Sangh") in a resolution of its central executive meeting.[227]

Other governmental statements regularly used vocabulary and phrases that subscribed to the Hindu version. For example "affected areas" for regions where a change of religion took place, and such formulations as "ordered to prevent any further occurrences. . . ." The official partisan sentiments were blatantly reflected in a home ministry letter. Referring to the conversion of Muslims to Hinduism in Rajasthan, the letter says: "[They] have reaffirmed their faith in Hinduism. . . . No instance of inducement. . . bringing about such reaffirmation of faith has come to the notice of the government." On the other hand, the same letter asserted "conversion" in Tamil Nadu to be ". . . influenced by the lucrative employment in Arab countries. . . ." The letter went on reassuringly that ". . . all precautionary measures have been taken to prevent *Adi Dravidas* (Tamil untouchables) being converted to become Muslims."[228]

One may dismiss the official rhetoric of reaction, considering it a political necessity in response to the majority constituency opinion. But gradually the political leadership became involved in the symbolic activities that resembled what Hindu revivalists were doing themselves. Prime Minister Mrs. Gandhi made a point of visiting every Hindu temple during her extensive travels, taking good care of the publicity side. She put Christian missionaries on notice when she presided over the inauguration of the Rajarajeshwari Tripurasundari Temple in Madhya Pradesh flanked by two of the *Shankaracharyas* (The highest priesthood in Hinduism).[229] The government-run television has also been found projecting Hindu views with "the zeal of an evangelist."[230] In another gesture to appease the Hindu majority, Mrs. Gandhi directed chief ministers to enforce the ban on cow slaughter more vigorously. She also commended the suggestion of Acharya Vinoba Bhave (a leading Hindu figure) that some "social" workers strongly opposed to cow slaughter should be associated with the enforcement of the ban.[231]

The official reaction went further than rhetoric and symbolism. It started taking steps not in the best spirit of the official secularism so vehemently guarded by Mrs. Gandhi's father, the late Prime Minister Nehru. Despite the fact that the constitution of India guarantees complete freedom to profess, practice, and propagate a faith, the government of India became actively involved in preventing conversions. The Home Ministry's letter about taking "precautionary measures" to prevent conversions have already been mentioned. These intentions and a government plan of action were confirmed later in detail.[232] They manifested themselves at different levels. In one incident, responding to the call of Dalit Panthers (an untouchable organization) that some twenty-five thousand untouchables would forsake Hinduism in a mass conversion on August 15, 1981 at Kanpur, Utter Pradesh, the state government prohibited the public meeting of the Dalit Panthers and arrested their leadership prior to the conversion day. A Home Ministry report approvingly mentioned this incident: "As a result of the precautionary measures taken by the state government, the threatened mass conversion at Kanpur did not take place."[233] According to a leading journalist, the Prime Minister secretly met Hindu religious leaders and asked for the mobilization of the masses to initiate government intervention.[234] The Union Home Ministry also suggested that the states enact laws to curb conversions on the pattern of existing Orissa and Madhya Pradesh laws, which have successfully restricted the Christians' missionary activities in these states.[235] Responding to the demand of Hindu revivalists and the popular image of the involvement of "Gulf money" in the conversions,[236] the central government barred several organizations from accepting foreign financial contributions without prior permission of the government under section 5(1) of the Foreign Contribution (Regulation) Act.[237] The main target of these actions was Christian missionaries.

This study does not attempt to deal extensively with the whole magnitude of reaction and backlash in the aftermath of conversion, as this epiphenomenon is itself a topic for the student of secularism in reference to Indian public institutions and the political culture. The significant points left out of this brief discussion are reaction of the intelligensia, of the media, of opposition parties, and of other minority groups. Nevertheless, the main features of the epiphenomenon have been presented. It is still difficult to depict the injury that the majority community feels it has experienced at the hands of an "out caste" community whose condition, it believes, it has helped so much to improve. If the reaction is considered a measure of the effectiveness of conversion, this protest by the untouchables turned out to be a telling action on behalf of their dignity and interests.

11

Conclusion

Reflections on the Historical Debate About Conversion to Islam

Three main themes emerge from the works of the historians and social scientists who have studied the spread of Islam in India:

Coercion Thesis

According to this view conversions were a result of Muslim conquest and subsequent physical coercion, accompanied by political coercion and socio-economic compulsion.[238]

Rewards Thesis

This rather moderate view considers that people of lower caste as a matter of convenience eventually adopted the religion of their masters as a matter of convenience, and that it was the possibility of material rewards that attracted the poor.

Social Mobility Thesis

This thesis emphasizes the voluntary nature of conversions and suggests that lower castes became Muslims to free themselves from oppression and raise themselves in social scale. This process was accelerated by the effort of sufi teachings or personal charisma. It was thus Islamic egalitarianism that allured people.

T.W. Hunter and Sir Alfred Lyall are among the prominent scholars who dispute interpretations that stress coercion. T.W. Arnold attributes conversion to Islam to the charismatic sufis.[239] Still others suggest that incentive and coercion both play a role. Untouchables, in accepting conversion, were often responding to the "appeal of an egalitarian religion preached by the powerful." Prof. Ishtiaq Qureshi, on the other hand, offers the most sophisticated explanation of the peaceful acceptance hypotheses. He thinks that conversion to Islam in South Asia was more the eventual outcome of a process which sometimes extended over several generations. This process, in Hardy's words, "began as a loosening, rather than an abandoning, of old religious and social ties."[240] In Sind, Kashmir, and Bengal the process was facilitated by the hostility of the Buddhist masses towards the dominant Hindus. The process continued by further Islamization efforts of the Muslim missionaries and over centuries resulted in the formation of Muslim majorities in these areas. In the case of South India and Mewat, however, this process of gradual and indirect conversion remained inconclusive in the shape of "half-way houses towards the acceptance of Islam" like Malkanas community. In the case of South India, Prof. Qureshi thinks that, due to lack of organization, Muslims failed to tap the possibilities of conversion offered by the favorable social situations.[241]

All these theses, however plausible they might be, suffer from lack of evidence. The relevant source material is meager. It is based on historical accounts compiled by the not-so-objective historians and selectively used by scholars in a period when the communal politics of India was drawing its argument from history as well as from the numerical strengths of the communities. This is the politics of history and the background of communal competition in India which have generated more heat in the aftermath of recent conversions than the number of converts might have warranted. Nevertheless, the debate around the recent conversions has provided a unique opportunity to test some of these hypotheses. It has produced information about all the relevant aspects which, scholars have complained, were lacking in the case of historical debate.

Of course, today's setting is completely different from the historical scenario. In independent India "preaching by the powerful" no longer exists. Muslims in India are anything but a dominant political power there, and Hinduism is not a common name for the thousands of unrelated, scattered sects but a religion of a thriving nationalism with the bitter memory of a perceived thousand years of subjugation. This change of political scenario, while it eliminates the coercion variable from the analysis, puts the other hypotheses—social mobility, religious merit of a peaceful and voluntary nature—to an even tougher test, since these conversions have occurred in an adverse power situation. The conversions under study, as earlier chapters have discussed, do not support coercion or reward theses. They do, however, show some evidence that it was partly an effort for social mobility, while being in essence a protest.

The process of the conversions under study, on the other hand, bears a striking resemblance to Prof. Qureshi's formulation of the spread of Islam in South Asia, although on a smaller scale. Conversion in this case did start with the loosening of the grip of Hinduism as a result of anti-Brahmin movement and the Dravidian ideology. Increases in social tension provided the basic stimuli for actions, and in this scenario the contrast of egalitarian Muslim community with the Hindu practice of untouchability made a choice for those who were already at distance with Hinduism. Many converts mentioned that the idea of conversion was long considered in their families. Lack of Muslim missionary organization, however, is partially responsible for the slower pace of conversion.

Who is Responsible for the Missionary Activities in Islam?

A majority of the studies on conversion to Islam focus on locating "someone," who is converting people. In the tug of war between those who consider coercion the main factor in the spread of Islam and those who piece together evidence of peaceful communication, converts are not given much attention by either side. Both search for "converters," in the absence of organized missionary activity in Islam. Those who find coercion theses more plausible name some sultan, caliph, or army leader roaming around converting people. Others, in opposition to the coercion thesis, have posited Muslim merchants, sufis, and ulama doing it.[242]

This search for individual "converters" may be due to the fact that these studies are done by historians about the period when history was written as rulers' biographies. Thus, the scope of research was limited to this sort of evidence. But these scholars could still have asked the question why one sufi rather than another was interested in converting people? Why some kings, army chiefs, merchants, ulama gave priority to preaching Islam while others in the same profession did not?

Kings, as is evident from treaties on their duties; sufis, as is clear from the *Malfuzat*; and ulama, as a study of *Dars-e-Nizami* would reveal; were not assigned duties of converting people to Islam.[243] Then why would some of them indulge in spreading Islam or converting non-Muslims? To ask a rather basic question, who in fact is supposed to convert people in Islam?

Although treatises on government, *Malfuzat*, and *Dars-e-Nizami* are silent about it, they in all likelihood frequently—if not daily—read the Quran, as is the practice of pious Muslims. It is quite likely that those kings, sufis, and merchants who became instrumental in the spread of Islam in different parts of the world were influenced by their reading of Quran, which makes it the duty of every Muslim to communicate the message of Islam to non-believers. The term *Shahadah* ("being witness") is used in the Quran to describe this assignment:

> O believers. . . struggle in the way of God as ought to be struggled in His way. He has chosen you, and He has not laid on you in your religion any constriction. Follow the way of your father, Abraham. He has named you Muslims, before and in this, so that the Messenger would be witnesses before you, and you would be witnesses before all mankind. . . .[244]

It is not possible for a social scientist to assess precisely how Quranic instructions were understood and acted upon through centuries. But since *shahadah* is a major recurring theme in Quran regarding the purpose and duties of Muslim individuals and *ummah*, it is quite likely that believers were inspired by it. This is the only plausible explanation of why some sufis, but not all, some kings and some merchants, but not all, possibly became instrumental in spreading Islam. This individual inspiration may be the only difference between the kings Shah Jahan (1627-1658) and Aurangzeb (1658-1707). Aurangzeb was interested in the spread of Islam while Shah Jahan was not, although both were Mogul kings with the same background.

In the case of conversion in Tamil Nadu under study, however, initiative was in the hands of untouchables who accepted Islam. Therefore, a search for some ''converter,'' like petro-dollars is unwise. The new Muslims were, nevertheless, in contact with established Muslims. Some of these Muslims helped them, be they from Jama'at-e-Islami, Tabligi Jama'at, or Muslim League, while others did not, as noted in an earlier chapter. But none of these groups are missionary organizations, dedicated to preach Islam to non-Muslims. It is safe to conclude, therefore, that Muslim individuals, inspired by their personal Islamicity, have been instrumental in the spread of Islam in the absence of any organized missionary activity.

Changing Nature of Conversions from Social Mobility to Protest

Religious conversions were part of both the pre-independence and the post-independence phases of the untouchable struggle. In the pre-independence phase, conversions were to Christianity, and mainly for the purpose of social mobility. But it is the conversions in modern India which have had an obvious protest nature. The neo-Buddhist movement suggested the complexity of cultural, ideological, and political meanings embodied in the act of conversion. This conversion of a relatively advanced mobile community of untouchables can be regarded as a strategy for seeking dignity by continuing a ''negative relation ship'' with the dominant Hindu society. Ambedkar opted for Buddhism as a religion other than Hinduism; it symbolized a token protest and provided an identity outside Hinduism. This protest, however, was a sophisticated choice of a sober national leader who responded to his sharp discontent by embracing a religion known for its tolerance.

This study has argued that today, in the current phase of the untouchables' struggle, they are more intensely discontented as a result of their perception of relative deprivation. In recent years, these untouchables have acquired a relatively better economic and educational position. Perceiving themselves as equal in these respects to caste Hindus, they now aspire to equal social status and treatment, which are being denied to them by the society. The administrative apparatus (especially the police) is disproportionately responsive to the dominant local castes, because of their political power and capacity to maneuver. Hence, neither is the society, traditionally dominated by higher castes, changing its norms to accommodate the aspirations of these untouchables, nor are administrative/judicial remedies easily available to pursue grievances against the dominant caste. In addition, the state machinery has its limitations in dealing with the complexities of human behavior and attitudes. This frustration of their aspirations is one of the important instigating determinants of anti-system aggression among untouchables in general. They are angered because they feel they have no means for attaining new or intensified expectations, which are nothing less than equality.

Different mediating factors have, however, led this aggressive behavior to different manifestation. A general increase in the violence involving untouchables is one of the less sophisticated manifestations of the untouchables' unorganized individual aggression, which is also sometimes used for deterrence and retaliation. The activities of the Naxalite movement and the Dalit Panthers, on the other hand, are the organized manifestations of aggressive behavior.

In the conversion manifestation of this aggressive behavior, the mediating factors are found in the local Tamil Nadu environment. The anti-Brahman and the rationalist movement, Dravida Kazagam and DMK, all had an anti-Brahmanical Hinduism slant in their ideology. This helped focus Hinduism as a target in the perceptions of untouchables.

The objective determinant (cause), socio-economic equality contrasted with relative deprivation in everyday life, were translated by the untouchables' socially and spatially mobile elite into the reasons for conversion, in the wake of the immediate incidences of police/Thevar oppression. The well-known option of conversion facilitated the task of these leaders in leading their fellows to that alternative. Social contact with Muslims and the availability of Islamic literature were also, to varying degrees, among the mediating variables for the selection of Islam. In the presence of Thevars' oppressive behavior and police harassment, this "exit" (as Hirschman uses the word) from Hinduism became a conscious and articulate rejection of an unjust order.

The selection of Islam reflects a more intensive discontent than the Ambedkar movement. No other religion and community is perceived, dogmatically and historically, as diametrically opposed to Hinduism and Hindus as Islam and the Muslims in India. In adopting Islam, untouchables have expressed their contempt for Hinduism and hostility to Hindus. In this reaction, untouchables are close to the Black Muslims' rejection of "white Christianity" in the U.S.A.[245] Protest and "psychological violence," then, is the major determinant in the decision to reject one religion and opt for another. In this form, this is a symbolic restoration of dignity and an assertion of independence.

One of the rational goals of this action is "demonstration of will and capability of action." Although the concept of protest denotes a condition of being against something, it also includes being for something else. One is also likely "to make calculations, whether shrewd or self-deceiving, about the gains we can achieve through aggressive action."[246] In our case the calculation seems a shrewd one, keeping the egalitarianism and the good socio-economic status of Tamil Muslims in mind.

Socio-economically, these converts were not in a situation of absolute deprivation or oppression. Most of these people, like Ambedkar, were in the highest stratum of untouchables, educationally and economically. Thus, they were more sensitive than oppressed. Their perception of deprivation was greater than their material deprivation.

Personally, most of them have benefitted from government's progressive discrimination policies and have achieved a status better than the general lot of their fellows. But this has not disconnected them from their community. Their discontent is as much based upon the historical sense of injustice and on the plight of their community as on their personal past experiences. That is why this study considers the personality revealed in the conversion a "little Ambedkar," who, although not necessarily a nationwide leader or a caste leader, felt the same way and tried to lead his neighborhood in the direction of his thinking. There are thousands of these personalities among untouchables today. Behind every assertion we can find one of them.

Although this study has gone into the details of the specific local environment and conditions of decision which mediated the discontent into a particular form of action and has substantiated it with the subjective opinions, one can still ask why the majority of untouchables in Tamil Nadu did not act the way a few thousand did, while they also live in the same environment and situation? This is indeed an important question which has many answers. It is correct that only few thousand have converted, but a number of untouchables would have duplicated the action if it had not been partly contained by the backlash of the Hindu community. Continued conversions on a limited scale support this position.[247] Although not a substantial number of untouchables have accepted Islam as religion, untouchables as a community have come closer to the Muslim community. An untouchable/Muslim front, *Samathuva Sahodaratha*

Sangam ("Association for Equality and Brotherhood—SSC") has been formed to confront the activities of Hindu revivalists jointly. The organization is becoming popular in the area.[248] Some are afraid that it is a preface to another conversion wave, since it is functionally equivalent to conversion. It satisfies the same kind of rebellious behavior and has the same effects on its caste opponents. Another answer to the question posed is that conversion is just one manifestation of the rebellious behavior of Tamil untouchables. Increasing Naxalite episodes and communist mobilizations of agricultural laborers are other outlets. Those who demonstrate in this behavior, whatever its form, are part of a stratum of untouchables which in itself is a smaller category. Finally, it should be noted that most discontented individuals are not revolutionaries. They may be angry, but they tend to prefer peaceful means for the attainment of their goals.[249]

The question why a majority of Afro-Americans did not participate in the ghetto riots of the 1960s in the U.S.A. is still open to a more sophisticated theoretical explanation. But as Locke's formulation of tacit consent suggests, the legitimacy of conversion is confirmed by nonparticipants' explicit approval or implicit condoning of their action, which exists because of the similarity of their discontent. No untouchable leader in Tamil Nadu or outside the state, including the best known untouchable leader, Jagjivan Ram, has condemned this conversion. Rather they have tried to justify or rationalize it.[250]

Although the current aggressive behavior of untouchables has many manifestations, its main characteristic, evident in conversions as well as in other instances, is that it lacks a charismatic personality and organizational structure which can channelize and coordinate the energy generated by sporadic assertiveness and localized mobilizations. Due to its nature, this aggressiveness, it seems, will continue without turning into any larger untouchable movement. It is, nevertheless, quite likely that these "little Ambedkars" may find any national movement attractive in future if its agenda is suitable to their purposes.

The available theories on protest and psychological aggression, discussed in the Introduction, are generally successful in explaining the instigating variables, with the exception of Gurr's work, which is helpful in explaining mediating variables as well. But the explanation of any micro-event is so closely related to the actors' consciousness and their meaning systems that it becomes very difficult to be accurate merely by defining the objective societal instigating and mediating factors. Here the subjective component of evidence, which has not been given importance in the literature, becomes crucial.

Appendix One

A Note on the Studies
of Social Stratification
Among Indian Muslims

Many scholars, in their socio-anthropological studies of Indian Muslims' social stratification, have mentioned that their Muslim respondents generally deny the existence of caste among them,[251] although these scholars have observed it to be present. This non-acceptance of the "empirical reality" of caste by Muslims may actually be based on the doctrinal egalitarianism of Islam, or it might be in part based on Muslims' perception that admission of the caste status among them will damage their claim of egalitarianism in contrast with Hindus. Whatever the reasons, the curious point here is the response of the social scientists. Scholars such as Mines (1972), seem to have been influenced by this doctrinal and verbal pressure as well as by the real egalitarianism of Tamil Muslims, whereas researchers such as McGilvray (1974) have been perturbed by this "normative pressure," and have considered it a research problem. Faced with the same situation, some—such as Siddiqui and Bhattacharya (1973)—have tried to substantiate the presence of caste among Muslims from indirect and secondary evidence. But no one has properly addressed the rejection of present empirical reality itself. Like good anthropologists, they have penetrated into this wall of denial without questioning the phenomenon of denial. Hence, they have failed to give proper weight to this behavior as a variable keeping the social stratification of Indian Muslims in a state of flux.

This omission in studies of Muslim social stratification has apparently been influenced by the prevailing approaches in Hindu caste studies. These caste studies—since independence in India, and particularly since the early sixties—have moved away from accepting doctrinal varna models as a framework for studying caste and have emphasized the empirical approach, unlike the British ethnologists who accepted the "sacred sociology of traditional Hindu text."[252] Keeping in mind the nature of the Hindu religion as an ever-changing social reality, the principle of drawing simplifications from empirical work about the nature of caste and Hinduism (religion as well as society) is a valid research method. But the same anthropological "snapshot"will not be as useful in determining Muslims' behavior and attitude because of Islam's doctrinal nature. The dynamics of the position of doctrine in Islam determines its greater importance in studying Muslims as compared to the importance of Hindu sacred text in studying the Hindu social system. In Islamic history, there has hardly been a period when Muslim society of any region achieved the doctrinal height of egalitarianism. But striving towards these ideals has itself exerted tremendous influence on given social situations. Thus any study dealing with Muslims' social behavior must regard their verbal or doctrinal emphasis as a determinant in itself. This may be the reason that many social researchers have problems in interviews with Muslims, who tend to hide the hierarchical structures of Muslims' subdivisions in North India simply because they do not like its presence. This dislike is an important stimulus to social action.

Doctrinal basis aside, any message conveyed so consistently will have a twofold impact: one on the audience it is directed to and the other on the rhetoricians themselves, in time they will become convinced of the point they are attempting to convey. Practically, the audience will increasingly judge them by the standards of their statements. This whole process will not only have effects on perceptions, but will inspire changes in social reality as well.

For studying Muslim social stratification, it is necessary to take into account the respondents' subjective opinions and try to answer questions raised by their contrast to the objective situation. For example, what are the dynamics of this denial? How common is this? Is there any correlation between this denial and the socio-economic position of the respondent? Does this response correspond with respondent's practice of his religion? Or is it merely a function of his belief? Or is it a conscious tactic to distinguish his community from the Hindus'? Social conflict at the communal level may be more a reason than the influence of doctrinal egalitarianism, or it may be at least a complementary cause of the denial.

Students of Muslim social stratification, on the one hand, have overadopted the empirical, non-doctrinal emphasis of caste studies, whereas, on the other hand, some of them have continued to be influenced by the abandoned use of the varna model. On the pattern of varna or *dwija* dichotomy they use the words *ashraf* and *ajlaf* to categorize Muslim jatis, ethnic groups or tribes within them.[253] This theoretical dichotomy has no empirical basis at all. Unlike *varna* or *dwija*, which are well known, these terms are absolutely unknown to Indian Muslims in this context. The word *ashraf* is commonly used as a first name, and *sharif*, from the same root, as an adjective. But the word *ajlaf* does not exist even as a word among the Muslim masses.[254] One scholar has even "Islamized" the term *sanskritization* as *ashrafization* (Vreede-de-Steurs, 1969). There is no objection to borrowing terms or benefitting from the caste studies of Hindu society. But one should be careful in stretching the similarities. Otherwise, it might amount to reducing the sociological studies of Indian Muslims to what Dumont calls a "conformist catechism."[255]

Another crucial point missed by these scholars is the fundamental difference between the Muslims' highest "caste," *Sayyad*, and *Brahmin*. Unlike Brahmins, Sayyads do not have any kind of monopoly on religious leadership. Not only do they not control any religious institutions, but those who normally become religious leaders, e.g., *imam* or *Khateeb* or *Maulavi*, predominantly come from the economically lowest stratum of Muslim society. These who dominate the communication channels of Muslim mosques, in contrast to the Brahmins, usually belong to what these scholars call *Ajlaf*. It is mostly the poor people who send their children, orphans, and blind persons to madrasa (the only institutions producing imams and Maulavi). These mosque-attached institutions provide religious education along with free lodging, food, books, and clothes. Although being an imam does not convert a poor man into a prosperous one, it does at least assure a regular supply of food (or salary in urban areas) and social prestige. Their socio-economic background is reflected in their *juma Khutba* (weekly sermon during Friday prayer service), when they emphasize egalitarianism in reference to prophet Muhammad and *Khilafat* (caliphate, considered to be the ideal Muslim government) times. *Ulama* politicians have even invented a political slogan: *Masawat-e-Muhammadi* ("egalitarianism of Muhammad''). The socio-economic background of the religious leadership in South Asian Islam, therefore, affects the direction of social change in Muslim society in favor of increased egalitarianism. The dynamics of this difference in the institutional positions of Brahmin and Sayyad in reference to caste and social stratification have also gone unnoticed in the available studies.

Appendix Two

Ambedkar's Conversion as a Mild Protest

The nature of Dr. Ambedkar's discontent and of untouchables' anger today is the same. His well-known announcement, "I will not die a Hindu," was a protest. The difference in these two cases, however, is the level of discontent and protest. Today the anger is higher and the protest is sharper.

Ambedkar was sharp in his criticism of Hinduism and in the language of protest (his announcement of leaving Hinduism). But like a mature politician, he turned softer when it came to the action of protest (conversion to Buddhism). He announced a strong action of defiance and put forth high demands for his community, but settled down after reasonable bargaining. (Another example of this style is in the separate electorate issue.) His position as a national figure and as an undisputed leader of untouchables, and his training as an academician, resulted in a personality that could channel his own anger and discontent into sober manifestations. Thus his opting for Buddhism was least hurtful to Hindu sentiments. His decision was a mild and symbolic act of protest. Nevertheless, as a shrewd politician he announced his decision to convert two decades earlier than the actual conversion, using the announcement as a bargaining strategy.[256]

As a national leader and father of the constitution, he knew the limitation of his options. "What the consequences of conversion will be to the country as a whole. . . is well worth bearing in mind. Conversion to Islam or Christianity will denationalize the depressed classes.''[257] At the times of Ambedkar's announcement and his actual conversion, the political environment was very communal. Christianity was attached to the colonial power and Islam to the "separatist" Muslims. This situation gave Ambedkar a strategic advantage, but at the cost of limiting his options.

Also, ''if one is to decide intelligently how to act, a person must predict how others will behave. If he seeks to influence them, he needs to estimate how they will react to the alternative policies he can adopt.''[258] Ambedkar could not afford to antagonize the majority community to the extent of accepting Islam or Christianity in the nationalist/communal atmosphere of the pre- and post-independence periods. Some scholars have noticed the responses of Moonje, Savarkar, Shankaracharya, Kurtakoti, and Gandhi, whose communication clearly had shown Ambedkar the probable repercussions of his options.[259] He had to keep the interests of his community in mind. A sharper and more antagonistic level of protest might have undermined the future prospects of social mobility for his community with the first government of free India. Thus, if today's proponents of sharper protest have opted for conversion to a community which can offer better egalitarian treatment and status, Ambedkar made his protest milder for the sake of economic advantage to his community. The cause of social mobility was kept in mind by both protest conversions.

Appendix Three

Women in the
Conversion Process

The issue of the role of women in the conversions is a curious one. There are no data detailing the number of women who have converted to Islam in all the villages discussed in this study. The available data about one village, however, show that 42 percent of those who converted were women. This percentage is based on a name-list of new Muslims in Kurayur Village between February 27 and May 2 of 1980 provided by a correspondent of an Indian daily. This and other reports suggest that these conversions were mainly actions either of man-led households or of individual men. No report mentioned any individual women converts. This scenario is typical of other manifestations of untouchables' assertiveness, where women are not in evidence. The situation, though strange to a westerner and disliked by upperclass feminists in cosmopolitan India, is the way of life in the countryside, where more than three-fourths of Indians live. It would be, however, naive to assume that women played no role in the decision-making process conducted by men. Unfortunately, the enormous body of news, views, reports, and essays produced by the Indian newspapers and journals, including the official *Meenakshipuram Report*, did not attempt to look into women's role in the conversions. Is it because there was none, or is it due to the fact that almost all the army of reporters, investigators, and officials which invaded the area were men?

It is not conceivable that a decision as far-reaching as conversion was taken alone by men without consulting women in the family. Indeed, the first incident of conversion to Islam in Meenakshipuram involved a young couple. When an untouchable man married a caste Hindu (Thevar) woman, it created tension among the communities. They were asked to leave the village by untouchable elders. They fled to the neighboring state of Kerala, became Muslim, and came back to live in a nearby village. The husband remained in communication with the original community, and played a role in the conversion of Meenakshipuram. Nevertheless, none of the investigators interviewed the woman about her opinions on untouchability, about her rebellious disregard of caste regulations, or about the indifference to the feelings of her Thevar caste displayed in her marrying an untouchable. No one has even asked her husband about her opinions. But it is highly likely that this young lady and her courageous spouse reached the decision jointly, and then risked their lives by coming back to the area to influence others instead of living happily ever after elsewhere. Anthropological tools would be better suited, however, for looking into the role of women in the conversion process.

The *Meenakshipuram Report* itself supports the conclusion that women do not have a leadership role in India, be it in social institutions or officialdom. This report, prepared by the Office of the Director for Scheduled Castes and Scheduled Tribes, Government of India, Madras, provides a unique view of the whole spectrum of leadership which took part—from any side—in the events leading to conversion, in conversion itself, and in its aftermath. The investigators for this federal study were men. All ten government officers of the local administration who were interviewed for the official version of the events they observed, including all the police officers, were men. Both the newspaper correspondents who helped the investigators were men also. So the primary uninvolved—thus supposedly objective—sources did not include women, thereby limiting avenues of communication and access for this study to men only.

Similar is the case of the community leadership which met the visiting investigators in Meenakshipuram. All six members of the Hindu delegation, all six members of the new Muslim delegation, and all four Muslim representatives from the nearby localities were men. These delegations in all probability were true representatives of their respective communities. As is the practice in India, whenever it is a matter of representing a community or petitioning for it on the occasion of visiting higher-government officers, its members select their most prominent individuals.

All five office-bearers of the cultivating tenants' association, a modern organization, discussed in the report, are men. All eleven people who were allegedly part of a caste-untouchable feud preceded by conversion were men, according to the case registered by the police. All individuals, untouchable or caste Hindu, mentioned in the seven incidents of untouchability outlined in the report were also male.

The only woman named in the report, and the only one who came to see the investigators apparently on her own initiative, was an untouchable lady who complained of police harassment in the absence of her husband, who was wanted by the police.

Women, evidently, were not among the representatives of the communities. This, however, does not establish that they did not participate in family discussions of which we have no report. But considering that women suffer more from untouchability than men because of the traditional sexual liberties commonly taken by caste men, it is unlikely that women just went along without participating actively. Sexual harassment of untouchable women is the most prevalent and the least reported crime in Indian society. The fact that it is rarely registered with the police limits the value of official statistics. Suffice it to say that there are proverbs in more than one Indian language to the effect that untouchable women are available to everyone. Rape of untouchable women has recently become one of the major causes of untouchables' violent backlash.

There is, however, some evidence of female involvement in the conversion process. In at least one instance, a newspaper report mentioned Muslim women having been invited to untouchables' houses prior to conversion. There are photos showing untouchable women participating in conversion ceremonies, their heads covered with scarves in accordance with the Islamic dress code. There also exists a special madrasa for new Muslim women to teach them the basics of Islam. One sociologist has only this much to say: "Women began to change their way of life and started imitating the culture of Muslim women. . . . Thus. . . a cultural revolution started taking place."[260]

All evidence and lack of evidence considered, the author is of the opinion that women's participation in the conversion process is more "non-reported" than "non-existent." As far as women's position in the representative elite is concerned, because of the overwhelming evidence available, the only conclusion is that India as seen from Meenakshi-puram has yet to show some sign of women's active participation in the society.

Notes

Chapter 1

1. Rudolph and Rudolph have used this formulation and "unofficial civil war" to describe the widespread clashes among castes in the countryside of India. Lloyd I. Rudolph and Susanne Hoeber Rudolph, *In Pursuit of Lakshmi: The Political Economy of the Indian State*, (Chicago: University of Chicago Press, 1987) pp.7 & 390. I have stretched this usage to include religious violence as well.

2. H.R. Niebuhr's analysis and B. Wilson have made this kind of argument as discussed in Max Heirich, "Change of Heart: A Test of Some Widely Held Theories about Religious Conversion," *American Journal of Sociology* 83:656.

3. The Congress party led India into independence and has since ruled India except for three years. In 1969, the party split and the faction led by Mrs. Gandhi has since been called Congress Indira or Congress (I).

4. The increase is measured from the base figures of 1976. The minister of state for home affairs informed Rajiya Sabha on Feb. 25, 1982 that there were 26,748 incidents of violence against untouchables during 1980-81. This, compared to 1976 figures of 6,197 incidents of violence, is a more than fourfold increase over a five-year period. India, Office of the Commissioner for Scheduled Castes and Scheduled Tribes, *Report of the Commissioner for Scheduled Castes and Scheduled Tribes 1978-79*, 2 parts (Delhi: Controller of Publications, 1980), 1:231 (hereafter cited as *Commissioner 1978-79*). The 1980-81 data are as quoted in George Mathew, "Politicization of Religion: Conversion to Islam in Tamil Nadu," in *Political and Economic Weekly*, June 19, 1982, p. 1034, n. 48.

5. Although the Leninist-Marxist activists of the tribal-based Naxalbari movement of West Bengal were called "Naxalites" originally, in present use not everything under

the term "Naxalite" has a tribal base or a connection with the original movement. This term is used by different people for different meanings. Various groups of untouchables, with a formal name or without one, organized or semi-organized, which mobilize untouchables in order to assert their rights, and subsequently face violence or use it as a tactic, are generally branded by caste Hindu landlords and the law enforcement authorities as "Naxalites" in Bihar, Tamil Nadu, and some other states. (For Tamil Nadu "Naxalites," see *Indian Express* Magazine, Jan. 10, 1982, "Tamil Nadu's Police State.") In Bihar, the Naxalite movement did organize untouchables' violent mobilization but other groups such as "Khetiar Kisan Mazdoor Sangh" were merely branded "Naxalites." "To the landlords the Naxalites are those audacious untouchables who dare to question their hitherto unquestioned feudal authority and power." Jose Kananaikil, "Reaching Inward from the Periphery" (Ph.D. dissertation, University of Chicago, 1981), pp. 432, 436-7.

6. Peter H. Lindsay and Donald A. Norman, *Human Information Processing: An Introduction to Psychology* (New York: Academic Press,1972), p. 620.

7. Ivo K. Feierabend, Rosalind L. Feierabend and Betty A. Nesvold, "Social Change and Political Violence: Cross National Patterns," in *Anger, Violence, and Politics: Theories and Research,* ed. Ivo K. Feierabend, Rosalind L. Feierabend and Ted R. Gurr (Englewood, N.J.: Prentice Hall, 1972), p. 108.

8. Allen D. Grimshaw, "Interpreting Collective Violence: An argument for the importance of social structure," in *The Annals of The American Academy of Political and Social Science* 391 (Sept. 1970):9 (hereafter cited as *Annals*).

9. Austin T. Turk, "Social Dynamics of Terrorism," *Annals* 463 (Sept. 1982):127.

10. Alexis de Tocqueville, *The Old Regime and the French Revolution*, trans. Stuart Gilbert (Garden City, N.Y., 1955).

11. Ted Robert Gurr, *Why Men Rebel* (Princeton: Princeton University Press, 1970), p. 24. James C. Davies' hypothesis of a J-curve pattern of change goes a step further. It accounts not only for the frustration created by disappointed expectations in the present, but also notes estimates of the future. A more pessimistic estimate of the future strengthens the likelihood of violence. See James C. Davies,."Toward a Theory of Revolution," in *Anger, Violence, and Politics.*

12. Gurr, *Why Men Rebel*, p. 24.

13. Myron Weiner, "Political Participation: Crisis of the Political Process," in *Crises and Sequences in Political Development*, ed. Leonard Binder et al. (Princeton: Princeton University Press, 1971), p. 168.

14. Gurr, *Why Men Rebel*, p. 13.

15. Samuel P. Huntington, *Political Order in Changing Societies* (New Haven: Yale University Press, 1968), pp. 53-54.

16. Gurr, *Why Men Rebel*, p. 193. Gurr's use of instigating and mediating variables comes close to what Rudolph and Rudolph call objective and subjective determinants (causes and reasons). Rudolph and Rudolph's formulation is more comprehensive. It distinguishes both the determinants from each other and at the same time explains how they are linked. By objective determinants (causes) Rudolph and Rudolph refer to what "...social scientists as observers use to explain, predict or prescribe social action. Objective determinants, however, are distant and necessary, not proximate and sufficient conditions for social action...." Subjective determinants (reasons) are "...meaning and intention, the purposes, goals and values that inspire and orient actors and the calculations that they make about risks and costs in relation to the probabilities and

benefits of success attending proposed remedial measures." "Translating objective de-
terminants into subjective is the work of political leadership." Lloyd I. Rudolph and
Susanne Hoeber Rudolph, "Determinants and Varieties of Agrigarian Mobilization," in
Agrarian Power and Agrigarian Productivity in South Asia, ed. Meghnad Desai, Susanne H.
Rudolph and Ashok Ruda (Delhi: Oxford University Press, forthcoming).

17. I agree with Zimmerman's criticism that "Gurr uses only objective data and
does not measure subjective reactions for inferring psychological states of mind." It is
necessary to verify that "the researcher's definition of the situation is the same as the
definition of the subject." Ekkart Zimmermann, *Political Violence, Crises and Revolutions:
Theories and Research* (Cambridge, Mass.: Schenkman Publishing Co., 1983), pp. 63, 158.
In the absence of any sample-based opinion survey, I have used interviews of untouchable converts and non-converts for the subjective verifications of the objective analysis in
this paper (interviews conducted by me will be hereafter cited as "Interview").

18. H.L. Nieburg, *Political Violence: The Behavioral Process* (New York: St. Martin's
Press, 1969), p. 13.

19. Ibid., p. 77.

20. Albert O. Hirschman, *Exit, Voice and Loyalty: Responses to Decline in Firms, Organizations, and States* (Cambridge: Harvard University Press, 1970), p. 120.

21. Ted Robert Gurr, "Psychological Factors in Civil Violence," in *Anger, Violence,
and Politics,* p. 34. Gregory C. Elliot defines psychological violence as: "behaviors, or the
threat of behaviors, intended to humiliate, intimidate, or in other ways demean the
human dignity of another person or group in an attempt to coerce, curtail, or eliminate
their behavior." "Components of Pacifism: Conceptualization and Measurement,"
Journal of Conflict Resolution 24 (March 1980):27.

Chapter 2

22. *Report of the Backward Classes Commission,* First part (Delhi: Government of India, 1980) p. 56.

23. Ibid.

24. Another 7% of the Indian population categorized as scheduled tribes (52 million)
also suffer from untouchability.

25. Mark Juergensmeyer, *Religion as Social Vision: The Movement against Untouchability in 20th-Century Punjab,* (Berkeley: University of California Press, 1982), p. 24.

26. I have preferred to use a rather generic term, "untouchable," as it best focuses
on the problem without any such ideological package as the terms *Adi Dravida* or *Harijan*
have, and is still not as indifferent as "scheduled castes" to the plight of untouchables.
However, my choice is not made without some reluctance as I do not like to seem in
contempt of other human beings, as the equivalent Hindi word *achoot* is used scornfully
in India.

27. J. H. Hutton, *Caste in India: Its Nature, Function, and Origins,* (Cambridge: University Press,1946).

28. Marc Galanter, *Competing Equalities: Law and the Backward Classes in India,* (Berkeley: University of California Press, 1984), p. 15.

29. The constitutional safeguards and provisions for the development of scheduled
castes are found in various articles: *Educational safeguards* in Articles 15(4) and 29;

Employment in Articles 16(4), 320(4) and 333, *Social safeguards* in Articles 17 and 25; *Abolition of forced labor* in Article 23; *Protection from social injustice* in Article 46; *Reservation of seats in parliaments* in Articles 330, 332, and 334; *Promotion of educational and economic interests* in Article 46 and 275; and *Free legal aid* in Article 39A. India, Ministry of Law, Justice and Company Affairs, *The Constitution of India* (as modified up to August 1, 1977) (Delhi: Controller of Publications, 1978).

30. 467,712 in central government services, 300,208 in the public sector undertaking, 59,104 in the nationalized banks, 1,064 in government grant-receiving institutions, and 224,501 in the state service. (Figures do not include the data of twelve states.) These figures do not include sweepers, one of the traditional occupations of untouchables, *Commissioner 1978-79* 2:22-24, 81, 82.

31. 558,528 matriculates and above, + 894,710 below matric including illiterate untouchables were on the live register of employment exchanges as of 31st December, 1978. *Commissioner 1978-79*, 2:10.

32. To be exact, 8,101,567 persons. *Commissioner 1978-79*, 1:16.

33. 12.77% literacy among untouchables according to 1971 Census. 75.5% is the rate of primary school children. They are 14.78% behind the national literacy rate of 29.45% (1971) and 10.2% behind the national school-children rate of 85.7% in 1977-78. *Commissioner 1978-79*, 1:6.

34. Many scholars are critical of the preferential policies for untouchables on the grounds that side effects of these protective discrimination policies have been serious and that the system has elements of social control. Yet the crucial question is whether untouchables would have been able to achieve as much progress as they have in the absence of these policies. For criticism of the preferential policies see: Lelah Dushkin, "Scheduled Caste Politics"; Marc Galanter, "The Abolition of Disabilities"; and Eleanor Zelliot, "Gandhi and Ambedkar" in *The Untouchables in Contemporary India*, ed. J. Michael Mahar (Tucson, Arizona: University of Arizona Press, 1972).

35. Joan P. Mencher, "Continuity and change in an ex-untouchable community of South India," in *Untouchables in Contemporary India*, pp. 50, 52 (Tucson).

36. India, Office of the Commissioner for Scheduled Castes and Scheduled Tribes, *Report of the Commissioner for Scheduled Castes and Scheduled Tribes, 1977-78*, 2 parts (Delhi: Controller of Publications, 1979), 2:121 (hereafter cited as *Commissioner 1977-78*).

37. *Commissioner 1978-79*, 1:183. In Thanjavur district, however, only 19.51% of surveyed villages have this problem, maybe because Thanjavur has been the seat of various communist parties which are strong among untouchables. Nevertheless untouchability is practiced in 70.7% of the restaurants and hotels. Ibid.

38. *Commissioner 1978-79*, 1:231.

39. *Census of India 1981*, Series I, Paper 2 of 1981, p. 26; *Census of India 1981*, Series I, Paper I of 1981, p. 45; *Census of India 1971*, Series 1, Part II-C(i), pp. 162-3.

40. India, Central Statistical Organization; *Statistical Abstract India 1978*, New Series No. 23 (n.d.), pp. 23, 573, 522, 31, 512 respectively.

41. *Census of India 1971*, Series 19, Part II-C(i), pp. 66-67; *Census of India 1971*, Series 19, Part II-B(i), pp. 8-9.

42. See *Sunday*, April 3-19, 1983.

43. For a detailed discussion, see Robert L. Hardgrave, Jr., "The Breast-Cloth Controversy: Caste Consciousness and Social Change in Southern Travancore," in Robert L. Hardgrave, Jr., *Essays in the Political Sociology of South India*, (Delhi: Usha Publications, 1979), pp. 146-63.

44. The Brahminical concept of sanskritization as presented by Srinivas means emulation of higher caste norms and practices by lower castes. M.N. Srinivas, *Social Change in Modern India*, (Berkeley: University of California Press), 1971.
45. These movements and personalities are discussed in detail in Chapter Seven.
46. Marguerite Ross Barnett, *The Politics of Cultural Nationalism in South India* (Princeton: Princeton University Press, 1976), pp. 70, 263, 299, 300.
47. *Commissioner 1978-79*, 2:111.
48. *Statistical Abstract*, p. 262.
49. India, Ministry of Information and Broadcasting, *India: A Reference Annual 1980* (New Delhi: Publication Division, 1980), p. 470.
50. *Commissioner 1978-79*, 1:138-9 and 2:125-6.
51. Blue Supplement to the *Monthly Public Opinion Surveys* 19 (May 1974):IX.
52. *Commissioner 1978-79*, 2:138-140.
53. Claude Alvares, "Tamil Nadu's Police State," in *Indian Express*, Jan. 10, 1982, pp. 1, 4.
54. *Commissioner 1978-79*, 1:182-4. Period of the survey is not mentioned in the report. It is also necessary to note that the average of landless untouchables in these villages is 84.33% (calculated by me on the basis of data).
55. *Commissioner 1977-78*, 2:120.

Chapter 3

56. Ibid. 1:238.
57. It is difficult to determine, however, to what degree the increase is due to better reporting and what is a result of real increase in the occurrence of atrocities.
58. *Indian Express*, Nov. 20, 1981, April 18, 1982; *Hindu*, Jan. 27, 1982; *Statesman*, Nov. 23 & 24, 1981.
59. *Indian Express*, Jan. 24, 1982.
60. *Commissioner 1977-78* 1:143.
61. *Indian Express*, April 18, 1982; *Hindu*, Jan. 27, 1982; *Statesman*, Nov. 23, 1981.
62. *Commissioner 1977-78*, 2:129-133.
63. *Indian Express*, April 18, 1982.
64. Walter K. Andersen, "India in 1981," in *Asian Survey* XXII (Feb. 1982):131.
65. Eckehard Kulke, "Integration, Alienation and Rejection: The Status of Untouchables," in *Aspects of Changing India*, ed. S. Devadas Pillai (Bombay: Popular Prakashan, 1976), pp. 250-251. An all-India survey of untouchables also established this correlation of education and preference of violence: 41% of the educated (above high school) respondents supported violence for self-defence as compared to 15% of the illiterates. Blue Supplement to the *Monthly Public Opinion Surveys* 9 (March 1974) p. XII. An observer of the recent literary trends among untouchables also reports evidence that such revolutionaries as Mao Zedong, Che Guevara, Martin Luther King, and Malcolm X are often referred to and their lives are considered exemplary for the untouchables of India. Jayashree B. Gokhale-Turner, "Bhakti or Viroda," *Journal of Asian and African Studies* XV:1-2, 1980. p. 29.
66. Kulke, "Integration, Alienation and Rejection," pp. 249-250. In response to the question of who did more for the untouchables, the level of education made a great difference:

	Gandhi	*Ambedkar*
Illiterates	84.9%	0%
High School	61.0%	34.7%
Graduates	2.8%	70.8%

Ibid.,p. 251.

67. Mencher, "Continuity and Change," pp. 48-56

68. *Commissioner 1977-78* 1:143.69. Bharatia Janata Party, *The Meenakshipuram Report* (issued by Headquarters Gen. Secretary Tamil Nadu BJP, n.d.), pp. 10-11.

70. *Economic and Political Weekly*, April 24, 1982, p. 717; *India Today*, July 15, 1982, p. 22.

71. For the study of Nadar caste association in Tamil Nadu see Robert Hardgrave, Jr., *Nadars of Tamilnad: The Political Culture of a Community in Change*, (Berkeley: University of California press), 1969. Dr. Ambedkar was of the Mahar caste himself. See Appendix II for a note on Ambedkar's conversion.

Chapter 4

72. These observations are based on the study of Deoli, Sadhupur, Kestara, Belchi, Banta, Bider and Narainpur. All are major massacres and clashes of the last few years. The massacres of Deoli, Sadhupur, Kestara are studied by Abdul Malik (author of this work) in "Monthly Massacres of Untouchables," (Course paper, Department of Political Science, University of Chicago, 1982, typescript).

73. See Marc Galanter, pp. 154-159; also see India, Government of India, *Report of the Backward Classes Commission 1980*, 2 parts (Delhi: Controller of Publications, 1981), 1:56.

74. *Report of the Backward Classes Commission 1980*, 1:56, 92. These data sound even more extreme when translated into slogans by the political statements of the backward classes' leadership. They often say that a 10% minority (three high castes) is denying 90% of the people their share in the national wealth and the governance of the country. See *Muslim India* 48, December 1986, p. 561.

75. The backward castes' rivalry with untouchables is comparable to the findings that, in the USA, poor southern whites were more prejudiced against Afro-Americans than better-off whites. See Cantril, 1941 and Campbell, 1947 as quoted in Santokh Singh Anant, "Changing Caste Attitudes towards Harijans" in *Cohesion and Conflict in Modern India*, ed., Giri Raj Gupta, (Durham, 1978), p. 33.

76. This and the following from Government of Tamil Nadu, *Report of the Backward Classes Commission 1970*, 3 vol. (Madras: Director of Stationery and Printing, 1974), 2:28-29, 47-49 (hereafter cited as *Backward Classes Commission Tamil Nadu*).

77. Ibid., 2:124-5.

78. Robert K. Merton, *Social Theory and Social Structure* (New York: Free Press, 1963), p. 234, quoted in Barnett, p. 24.

79. Hardgrave, Jr., *The Nadars of Tamil Nadu*, pp. 114-120. Also see Rudolph and Rudolph, *The Modernity of Tradition: Political Development in India* (Chicago: University of Chicago Press, 1967).

80. *Backward Classes Commission Tamil Nadu*, 2:29, 48.

81. Rudolph and Rudolph, "Transformation of Congress Party: Why 1980 Was Not a Restoration," *Economic and Political Weekly* XVI (May 2, 1981):815.

82. In the anti-untouchable agitation of Gujarat, during January-February 1981, a few scholars recorded that out of a total of forty-seven incidents of damage to houses and properties, burning, looting, physical injuries, and death against untouchables, the police were involved with the caste Hindus in joint attacks twelve times. There were ten attacks exclusively carried out by the police. Achyut Yagnik and Anil Bhatt, "The Anti-Dalit Agitation in Gujarat," *South Asia Bulletin* IV:1, Spring 1984, pp. 45-60.

83. Bienen uses this formulation for defining police/Negro relationships by referring to Grimshaw and Hayden. Henry Bienen, *Violence and Social Change: A Review of Current Literature* (Chicago: University of Chicago Press, 1968), p. 34.

84. On occasion, this police/dominant caste axis against untouchables takes formal shape. One example of this occurrence is the so-called anti-Naxalite committees of landlords sponsored by police in Tamil Nadu to collaborate with anti-Naxalite cells of the police in dealing with the untouchable mobilization of landless laborers. *Indian Express*, January 10, 1982.

85. *Week*, August 1985, pp. 25-31. Paul Brass observed the same in the case of Uttar Pradesh. The untouchable leadership selected by congress for the reserved constituencies are generally non-militant and without a power base. Paul Brass, "Uttar Pradesh," in *State Politics in India*, (Princeton, 1968), p. 96. In electoral politics, Hardgrave argues, ". . . the fact remains that all castes do not have equal access to power." Robert L. Hardgrave, Jr., *India: Government and Politics in a Developing Nation*, (New York, 1980), p. 216.

Chapter 5

86. George Mathew, "Politicization of Religion," p. 1028.

87. Ibid.; the highest figure is given by Frabhu S. Guptara, "Harijan Conversion," *Arabia*, Dec. 1981, p. 33. No other reports supports this number.

88. *Meenakshipuram Report*, p. 17; S. Albones Raj, "Mass Religious Conversion as Protest Movement: A Framework," in *Religion and Society* XXVIII (Dec. 1981):60.

89. *Sunday*, June 7, 1981, p. 41. Another village, Annaikari-Patti in Madurai District, also resembles our villages of conversion socio-economically. Here 170 untouchables had become Muslim as of Feb. 1982. It is a 100% untouchable village with 400 families. They own nearly 200 water pump sets for their wells. Most of them are landowners, and have benefited from government loans. Three doctors hail from this village. They claim to be the most educated village in Madurai District. This village is considered leader of up to thirty other untouchable villages in the area. Andrew Wingate, "A Study of Conversion from Christianity to Islam in Two Tamil Villages," *Religion and Society* XXVIII (Dec. 1981), pp. 17-19.

90. Percentage above 100 denotes enrollment of an even higher age group who did not enroll in the previous years. *Commissioner 1978-79*, 2:132.

91. *Sunday*, June 7, 1981.

92. *Indian Express*, June 16, 1981.

93. *Sunday*, June 7, 1981.

94. Report of the conversion of two Meenakshipuram doctors appeared only in one letter to the editor in *Radiance*, August 9, 1981, p. 9.

95. *Radiance*, Sept. 7, 1980.

96. I have used the term "semi-leader" because in some cases, such as Meenakshipuram, the person who first proposed the conversion and then contacted Muslims was

not a traditional caste or political leader. (The headman of the untouchable village did not himself change his faith.) Nevertheless, these kinds of people have played a leading role in conversion and they are political leaders in the sense that they are ". . . specially motivated, endowed and skilled individuals with ideas and means for collective action." Rudolph and Rudolph, "Agrarian Mobilization." The presence of a large number of government employees among the converts is significant, as this wandering elite of untouchable bureaucrats provides the essential communication lines for untouchables in the absence of effective untouchable press. See Barbara Joshi, *Democracy in Search of Equality*, (Delhi, 1982), p. 122.

97. Interview.

98. *Sunday*, June 7, 1981, p. 43.

99. Robert Jervis, *Perception and Misperceptions in International Politics* (Princeton: Princeton University Press, 1976), p. 42.

100. Wingate, "Christianity to Islam," p. 6.

101. Raj, "Protest Movement," pp. 59, 61; *Meenakshipuram Report*, p. 25.

102. Wingate, "Christianity to Islam," p. 6.

103. Raj, "Protest Movement," p. 56.

104. Wingate, "Christianity to Islam," p. 6.

105. Mumtaz Ali Khan, "A Brief Summary of the Study on Mass Conversions of Meenakshipuram: A Sociological Enquiry," *Religion and Society* XXVIII (Dec. 1981), p. 44.

106. Wingate, "Christianity to Islam," p. 6.

107. Raj, "Protest Movement," p. 61.

108. *Meenakshipuram Report*, p. 24.

109. Ibid., p. 25.

110. *Sada-e-Saher*, Dec. 20, 1981.

111. Wingate, "Christianity to Islam," p. 9.

112. *Radiance*, Sept. 6, 1981.

113. Wingate, "Christianity to Islam," pp. 11-12.

114. *Commissioner 1977-78*, 2:119.

Chapter 6

115. Robert Redfield, *The Little Community* (Chicago: University of Chicago Press, 1955).

116. Mattison Mines, *Muslim Merchants: The Economic Behavior of an Indian Muslim Community* (New Delhi: Shri Ram Center for Industrial Relations and Human Resources, 1972), p. 7.

117. S.M. Sulaiman and M.M. Ismail, *Islam, Indian Religions, and Tamil Culture*, ed. Devasenapathi (Madras: University of Madras, 1977), p. 239.

118. *Census of India Report 1891*, as quoted in *Backward Commission Tamil Nadu*, 1:239.

119. Nora Mitchell, "Cultural Homogeneity in Tamil Nadu" (M.A. thesis, University of Chicago, 1963), pp. 38, 50, 56.

120. Mines, *Muslim Merchants*, p. 93.

121. Dennis B. McGilvray, "Tamils and Moors: Caste and Matriclan Structure in Eastern Sri Lanka" (Ph.D. dissertation, University of Chicago, 1974), pp. 244-245.

122. For Tamil Muslims' enthusiasm for the Khilafat movement see Arun Shourie, "Reasons for Hope," *New Quest*, July-August, 1982, p. 203. For Tamil Muslims' support for Tamil nationalism see Sulaiman and Ismail, "Tamil Culture," p. 46.

123. M. Srinivasa Aiyangar, *Tamil Studies: or Essays on the History of the Tamil People, Language, Religion and Literature*, First Series (Madras: Guardian Press, 1914), p. 187.

124. Mitchell, p. 37; Mines, *Muslim Merchants*, pp. 92, 104-5; *Backward Classes Commission Tamil Nadu*, 2:43.

125. *Backward Classes Commission Tamil Nadu*, 2:43. Beedi manufacturing has a cottage industry structure of production.

126. Mines, *Muslim Merchants*, pp. 22, 97; E. Kathleen Gough, "The Social Structure of a Tanjore Village," in *Village India: Studies in the Little Community*, ed. McKim Marriott (Chicago: University of Chicago Press, 1955), p. 43.

127. A Tamil Muslim businessman's first priority is to reinvest in his own business. Agricultural land comes as the fourth choice. In contrast, the ordering of desired investment among Hindu businessmen is agricultural land first; reinvestment in business ranks third. Mines, *Muslim Merchants*, pp. 93, 105.

128. "A Survey of Muslim Education in Tamil Nadu," in *Tamil Nadu Muslim Educational Conference*, 1973, Souvenir (Madras: Tamil Nadu Muslim Education Standing Committee, 1973). (No page numbers given, n.d., author not mentioned).

129. Mohammad Raza Khan, "Origin and Growth of Muslim Colleges in the South," *Tamil Nadu Muslim Educational Conference*, 1973.

130. Mines, *Muslim Merchants*, p. 100.

131. The Quran 51:19; 9:60. Scholars of Islamic economics, a growing field of research in the Muslim world, consider *zakat* to be one of the essential features of the "Islamic Economic System," resulting not only in the transfer of resources from the rich to the poor and to other welfare activities but in discouragement of hoarding and encouragement of circulation. See Muhammad Nejatullah Siddiqi, *Issues in Islamic Banking: Selected papers* (Leicester, UK: Islamic Foundation) 1983, pp. 16-18.

132. The following verse of Quran designates the recipients of *zakat*: "Alms are only for the poor and the needy and those who are employed to administer them; for those whose hearts have been recently reconciled (to the truth) and to free the slaves and the debtors and for the cause of God; and for the wayfarer. It is a duty imposed by God. God is full of knowledge and wisdom." *Quran* 9:60.

133. *Backward Classes Commission Tamil Nadu* 2:42.

134. There are two *Eids* which are the most important Muslim festivals. The one we are referring to here comes at the end of the fasting month. The other *Eid* is in commemoration of the prophet Abraham's symbolic sacrifice of his son. This one occurs at the end of *Haj* (pilgrimage to Mecca).

135. Individuals from the upper class and the urban elite normally are the members of Lions Clubs in India.

136. Mines' calculation on the basis of the Census of India 1961, *District Census Handbook for Madras*. Mines, *Muslim Merchants*, p. 8.

137. *Backward Classes Commission Tamil Nadur*, 2:43.

138. This relatively better representation for Tamil Muslims in government service is probably achieved with the help of quotas (reservations) for Tamil-speaking Muslims, because of their status as backward classes at the state level. Now this quota is available to all Muslims in Tamil Nadu, making them the only Muslim community besides Kerala who avail themselves of such preferential policies in India. Muslims in Tamil Nadu and Kerala are not the poorest of the Indian Muslims; it is rather their political strength which has brought them these benefits. See *Backward Classes Commission Tamil Nadu* 2:42; *for Kerala's rules governing reservations for the Muslim community see Muslim India* 46, October 1986.

Madras figures of 1962 for government service are taken from S. Saraswathi, *Minorities in Madras State: Group Interests in Modern Politics* (Delhi: Impex India, 1974), p. 142. Data for representation at the all-India level are taken from *Muslim India* 1 (Dec. 1983):552.

139. *Backward Classes Commission Tamil Nadu*, 2:42.

140. A member of the Backward Classes Commission traces the origin of the word "Labbai" to the Arabic word "Labbaik." Ibid., 1:236. This word means "here I am (O God)." It is used in the Quran as a metaphor for the general behavior of Muslims and is a popular word repeated by Muslims during Haj and in Eids.

141. Ibid., 1:240.

142. Mines, "Social Stratification among Muslim Tamils in Tamilnadu, South India," in *Caste and Social Stratification among Muslims in India*, ed. Imtiaz Ahmad (Delhi: Manohar, 1978), p. 162.

143. Imtiaz Ahmad, "Introduction," in *Caste and Social Stratification among Muslims in India*, pp. 3-4.

144. McGilvray, pp. 261, 263, 265, 272, 298. McGilvray, however, did find a very small group in Sri Lanka named Osta Vari which is ranked at the bottom, is endogenous and linked to a hereditary occupation. Only thirteen out of twenty-two Muslims stated their willingness to eat at the house of this group (Ibid., pp. 31-2). This exception does not constitute a problem for our case as this group does not exist in Tamil Nadu.

145. Mines, *Muslim Merchants*, p. 25. Also see Wingate, "Christianity to Islam."

146. McGilvray, p. 262.

147. One social scientist has noted that his respondents in Tamil Nadu were not "...concerned, that caste differences should disappear but rather that the castes should be 'the same'...it seemed that most village people interpreted the notion of 'equality' as meaning the removal of hierarchical distinction...." John Harriss, "Why Poor People Stay Poor in Rural South India," *Social Scientist* 8 (Aug. 1978):43.

148. See untouchables' interviews in Wingate, "Christianity to Islam."

149. Mines, *Muslim Merchants*, p. 32; Hardgrave, *Nadars of Tamil Nadu*, pp. 213-214, 225.

150. Hardgrave, *The Dravidian Movement* (Bombay: Popular Prakashan,1965), p. 73.

151. Mines, *Muslim Merchants*, p. 103. In the 1937 election the Justice Party had the highest number of its seats among Muslims (8), next only to the Muslim league (9). Christopher J. Baker, *The Politics of South India, 1920-1937* (Cambridge: Cambridge University Press, 1967), p. 311.

152. Muslim response in Tiruchirapalli is even 6% higher than the Hindu response in the city. Peter B. Mayer, "Tombs and Dark Houses: Ideology, Intellectuals and Proletarians in the Study of Contemporary Indian Islam," in *Modernization and Social Change Among Muslims in India*, ed. Imtiaz Ahmed, p. 31.

153. Catholics alone in India have about 9,045 educational institutions, with 3.5 million students. Around 4,000 foreigners also serve the Catholic missions in India. *Catholic Directory of India*, 1980, as quoted in Kananaikil, p. 79. Comparative figures for the Muslim community are not available, nor is a state-wide breakdown of these data.

Chapter 7

154. Although Brahmins constituted 3% of the population in Madras, during 1910-1920, eight out of nine Indians serving as official members of the Madras Legislative

Council were Brahmin. In the local government elections of 1916, ten elected members out of fifteen were Brahmins. Brahmins occupied 66% of the jobs in the judiciary and 79% in the educational departments, according to the data for the second decade of the twentieth century. In 1914, fourteen out of sixteen elected representatives of the Congress committee were Brahmins. The editors of the popular dailies were Brahmins also. S. Saraswathi, *Minorities in Madras State: Group Interest in Modern Politics*, (Delhi: Impex India), pp. 45-50. Also see Indhu Rajagopal, *The Tyranny of Caste: The Non-Brahmin Movement*. (Delhi: Vikas), 1985.

155. Hardgrave, *Dravidian Movement*, p. 30. Anti-Hindi campaigns are still common in Tamil Nadu. Recently, the president of DMK, M. Karunanidhi, along with 661 followers, served jail sentences. They were convicted under the Prevention of Insult to National Honour Act on charges of burning excerpts of the constitution as part of the DMK's Anti-Hindi agitation. *The Hindu*, Feb.3, 1987.

156. Anita Diehl, *E. V. Ramaswami Naicker-Periyar: A Study of the Influence of a Personality in Contemporary South India*, (Stockholm: Esselte Studium, 1977), pp. 41, 45.

157. Barnett, Tables 8-15. The current leadership of the different factions of the Dravidian movement, be it in-power ADMK, or under-reorganization DK, or in-opposition DMK, all occasionally still use the old ideological rhetoric. For example, DMK president M. Karunanidhi, in an article discussing the conversions, resorted to explanations which remind one of the Dravidian ideology as presented by its founder Periyar. *Sunday*, Nov.1, 1981.

158. Lloyd I. Rudolph, "Urban Life and Populist Radicalism," *The Journal of Asian Studies* XX (May 1961):288.

159. One public opinion survey supports this impression. Of the Hindu city dwellers in a Tamil city, 89% agreed that "any minority should be free to criticize majority decisions," as compared to 62% of the northern Hindu urbanites. Mayer, p. 21.

160. Translations from Tamil. No reference to the original source is given. As quoted in Maqbool Siraj, "Conversion to Islam in India," manuscript of a forthcoming book, 1980.

161. Hardgrave, *The Dravidian Movement*, p. 27.

162. India, Ministry of Home Affairs, *Bulletin for the National Integration Council*, May 16, 1969, p. 8, as quoted in Ratna Naidu, *Communal Edge to Plural Societies* (Delhi: Vikas, 1980), Table I, pp. 18-19. The national average is 249 per year if we compute it for the period 1957-1982. Average for the last five years (1979-1983) is, however, even higher—386 (excluding Assam). Ministry of Home Affairs Annual Report, 1983-84 on communal situation as quoted in *Muslim India* 2 (May 1984):202.

163. I am grateful to Prof. Norman Cutler, Dept. of South Asian Languages and Civilization, University of Chicago, for helping me understand the meanings of certain Tamil words.

164. Muhammad Nejatullah Siddiqi, "Tawhid: The Concept and the Process," in *Islamic Perspectives*, ed. Khurshid Ahmad and Zafar Ishaq Ansari (UK: Islamic Foundation) 1980, p. 18.

165. See Quran 2:167, 33:67, 34:31-33.

166. Quran 49:13.

167. Hadith.

168. Barnett, p. 89. This theme is not original to the Dravidian movement, which started with atheistic themes but by the late 1960s had moderated its anti-Hindu propaganda with the rhetoric of "One God One Caste." One finds this as a recurring theme in

the Bhakti literature, for example, Basavanna's lines: "The pot is a god/The winnowing fan is a god/The stone in the street is a god. . . . Gods, gods, there are so many/There's no place left for a foot/There is only one god. He is our Lord of the Meeting rivers." *Speaking of Siva*, translated by A. K. Ramanujan, (Penguin books), 1979, p. 28. More recently a reform movement in Tamil Nadu referring to Shastras asserted that "there was only one God. . . common to all whether they are high or low caste." Kudi Arasu, July 27, 1929 as quoted in Barnett, p. 33. In neighboring Kerala, Sri Narayana (−1928), guru of Ezhavas untouchables, also developed a new religious doctrine, "one caste, one religion, one God for man." Kananaikil, p. 123.

169. This environment has changed somewhat in the aftermath of conversion because of the Hindu communal mobilization in Tamil Nadu. Still, one public opinion survey (conducted during 1981-82) shows the difference in perception between Tamil people and people in other areas: "While none of the [350] respondents of Tamil Nadu including the Brahmins and the Thevars accept the theory of Gulf money, in Karnataka a majority of the Brahmins (69%) and the non-Brahmin upper caste people (65%) feel that mass conversions are due to Gulf money." In response to another question, "while a little more than two-thirds of all Brahmins only feel that mass conversions might disturb communal harmony, the rest of the Tamil Nadu either totally reject or marginally endorse the statement, and the majority of respondents of all groups of Karnataka entertain the possibility of communal tensions and conflicts." M.A. Khan, "Sociological Enquiry," pp. 49-50.

Chapter 8

170. Joseph Tharamangalam, "The Communist Movement and the Theory and Practice of Peasant Mobilization in India," *Journal of Contemporary Asia* 11:497

171. In Tanjore, an administrative district in Tamil Nadu which has a strong CPI-M presence.

172. The term "middle peasant" is functionally equivalent to "middle castes" or "other backward classes."

173. Ibid., p. 494.

174. This is another example of the police/dominant caste axis against untouchables.

175. *Indian Express*, January 10, 1982.

176. Rudolph and Rudolph, *Modernity of Tradition*, p. 187. The Rudolphs have, however, modified their position in their latest work. They explain the fragmented and small-scale "undeclared civil wars" in India today from a class perspective which focuses on the power position of the rural poor: "Divided from each other by economic interest and world view and facing larger, more powerful groups of self-employed independent cultivators and large landowners, the rural poor are not in a position to become a dominant, hegemonic, or revolutionary class. . . " Rudolph and Rudolph, *In Pursuit of Lakshmi*, p. 377.

177. Rudolph and Rudolph, *Modernity of Tradition*, p. 185.

178. Kananaikil, p. 118.

179. This tradition of foreign missionaries still continues, although on a smaller scale. There were more than 2,429 registered foreign missionaries in India in 1983. *Annual Report of Ministry of Home Affairs*, India, 1984-85, as published in *Muslim India* 29, May 1985, p. 198.

180. K. N. Sahay, "Indigenization of Christianity in India," *Man in India* 61:1, March 1981, p. 19.
181. Hardgrave, *Nadars of Tamil Nadu*, p. 91.
182. Brojendra Nath Benerjee, *Religious Conversion in India* (Delhi, 1982), p. 65.
183. Dhananjay Keer, *Dr. Ambedkar, Life and Mission* (Bombay: Popular Prakashan, 1962), p. 247.
184. For a current account of untouchability among Christians see: Wingate, "Christianity to Islam."
185. Sahay, p. 3.
186. Kananaikil, pp. 171-2.
187. Hardgrave, *Nadars of Tamil Nadu*, p. 117.
188. As quoted in Rabhu S. Guptara, "Harijan Conversion," p. 33.
189. See an article to that effect in the RSS official journal, *Organiser*, April 5, 1981.

Chapter 9

190. *Organiser*, June 21, 1981; the *Times of India*, March 21, 1981, issue also stated that a Muslim organization based in London had taken credit for the conversion of fifty families. The report also mentioned that this organization planned to convert half of the untouchable population and planned to send Urdu-speaking Arabs to Tamil Nadu for preaching. The selection of the Urdu language, however, itself reveals to what a small extent the concerned organization knows Tamil Nadu. There was no follow-up news of this kind in any other report in the paper.
191. *New York Times*, Aug. 1, 1982.
192. Other expenditures include needy students or travelers, orphans, widows, poor persons, debtors, and *Jihad* (holy war).
193. See Jerome J. Fussell, "Muslims' Methods of Propagating the Faith" (M.A. thesis, University of Chicago, 1949).
194. Amar Bhide, "India's Conflict Between Dirigism and Democracy," in *Wall Street Journal*, May 17, 1982, p. 27.
195. As far as legally received overseas contributions are concerned, none of the 21 Muslim organizations which receive foreign contributions, out of 143 named in the Indian government statement, are from Tamil Nadu. Ministry of Home Affairs in Lok Sabha on April 30, 1986, as quoted in *Muslim India* 45, September 1986.
196. *Meenakshipuram Report*, p. 25; Dr. Gopal Singh, chairman of the high-powered Commission on Minority, Government of India, also said in an interview with the author (November 4, 1982, Chicago) that according to government investigation there is no proof available to substantiate this charge. As far as the legal way of receiving foreign contributions is concerned, seven Muslim institutions as compared to 586 non-Muslim institutions in Tamil Nadu received the contributions during 1981-82. Amounts are not mentioned in the report. Lok Sabha unstarred question No. 9901 dated 4/28/82, as quoted in *Muslim India* 1 (Oct. 1983):444.
197. Hugh Tinker, *A New System of Slavery: The Export of Indian Labour Overseas*, (London: Oxford), 1974, p. 374.
198. Myron Weiner, "International Migration and Development: Indian in Persian Gulf," *Population and Development Review* 8 (March 1982), p. 32.

199. Tamil people generally do not have this perception because of their propinquity and their better understanding of the phenomenon. Also see Note 169.

200. Revision of history textbooks constitutes a major point of demands submitted by forty Muslim Members of Parliament to the prime minister of India in a memorandum on November 5, 1982. In the Janata government 1977-79 the prime minister's interest in proposing withdrawal of a few history textbooks which lacked "anti-Muslim and pro-Hindu enthusiasm" created a major controversy questioning the secularism of the Janata government. See Rudolph and Rudolph, "Rethinking Secularism: Genesis and Implications of the Textbook Controversy, 1977-79," *Pacific Affairs* 8 (Spring 1983). For the link between communal riots and history books, see Naidu, p. 103.

201. Nieburg, p. 78.

Chapter 10

202. Nieburg, p. 77.

203. See the following articles to grasp the strength of this shock: Ravindranath, "Some Home Truths," *Indian Express*, August 3, 1981; "The Challenge and the Response," *Indian Express*, August 10, 1981; Imtiaz Ahmad, "The Tamilnadu Conversions, Conversion Threats and the Anti-Reservation Campaign: Some Hypotheses," unpublished paper.

204. See "The Challenge and the Response," *Indian Express*, August 10, 1981; also see three letters to the editor in *Hindu* October 12, 27, and November 3, 1983 for a good appreciation of this "calculated" fear. The basis for this fear is an approximate 1% decadal decline in the proportion of Hindus in India. The proportion of Hindus in the Indian population was 84.98%, 83.50%, and 82.72% respectively in 1951, 1961, and 1971 Indian censuses. Conversion to Islam and Christianity, and Muslims' non-acceptance of birth control, and polygyny, are cited as causes of this change. Sociological studies, however, found that Hindus are slightly more polygynous than Muslims in India. In the case of polygynous marriages which took place during the ten years prior to the survey, 4.31% of Muslim as compared to 5.06% of Hindu marriages were found to be polygynous. The highest frequency of polygyny was found among tribals, followed by Buddhist and Jains. *Polygynous Marriages in India Survey, Census of India, 1971 Series 1-India*, Miscellaneous Studies, Monograph No. 4 (1961 series).

205. See *Organiser* June 21, July 19, 1981 for a glimpse of these types of statement.

206. Interview with Ram Dhan, former member of Lok Sabha and chairman of the Bharatiya Dalit Varga Sangh. *Onlooker*, October 16, 1981, p. 11. The number of converts claimed by neo-Buddhists was 20 million. The actual number is hard to calculate. See for discussion on this issue, Rudolph and Rudolph, *Modernity of Tradition*, pp. 137-8, 17n.

207. Imtiaz Ahmad, "Tamil Nadu Conversion."

208. *India Today*, September 1-15, 1981.

209. *Sunday*, November 1, 1981.

210. *Onlooker*, October 16, 1981, p. 11.

211. *Organiser*, June 21, 1981.

212. Ravindranath, "Some Home Truths," *Indian Express*, August 3, 1981; "The Challenge and the Response," *Indian Express*, August 10, 1981.

213. *Sunday*, June 27, 1982.

214. *Sunday*, April 3, 1983, p. 16. Ratna Naidu, p.18-9. *Sunday*, April 3, 1983, p.23. *Arabia*, July 1984, p. 10. For the relevance of this wave of riots to the conversions, see a special investigative report: "Revenge for Meenakshipuram," *Sunday*, March 14, 1982. It is about the February 1982 anti-Muslim riots in Pune. This riot, which erupted one year after the conversions, was the first of a long series in the first six months of 1982 in northern India.

215. *Indian Express*, July 24, 1984.

216. *India Today*, June 15, 1987.

217. *India Today*, August 15, 1986, p. 21.

218. *Sunday*, April 3, 1983, p. 27. There were 40,000 Muslims converted to Hinduism, according to Vishwa Hindu Parishad, 10,000 according to the police. *India Today*, June 30, 1986. For a Muslim view see a report of Jama'at-e-Islami, *Muslim India* 8, August 1983.

219. According to the southern *Hindu*, this reconversion movement added up to 300 Christians reconverting to Hinduism. *Hindu*, Nov. 15, Dec. 20, 1981, April 25, May 31, and June 14, 1982.

220. *Hindu*, February 11, 1982.

221. A three-dome mosque structure in Ayodhya established in AD 1526 by Babar, the founder of the Mughal empire. Hindus claim that it was the Ramjanmabhoomi Temple. This is an interesting example of the revivalist mobilization in which history is used as a symbol of an ongoing communal conflict. In AD 1885, some Hindus filed a claim in the British colonial courts that this mosque had been forcibly built by Muslims after demolishing a Hindu temple built on the birth site of their god Rama. The request for restoration was denied by the court on the grounds that the plaintiff had been unable to substantiate the claim. But the battle was not yet over. After India became independent, on Dec. 23rd 1949, the district magistrate of Faizabad (where this structure is located) informed higher authorities, "A few Hindus entered Babari Masjid at night when the Masjid was deserted and installed a deity there. . . Police picket of fifteen persons was on duty at night but did not apparently act." The district magistrate of Faizabad, Mr. Nayar, admitted his responsibility and was asked to resign. But soon after, Mr. Nayar was rewarded by the ruling Congress party with a seat in parliament (Lok Sabha). Instead of removing the idol and restoring the mosque to its custodians, the Sunni Waqf Board, it was locked and an official receiver, a Hindu, and a priest (also Hindu) were appointed to look after the place. Muslims, still suffering from the trauma of 1947, filed suit in the court—where it has been lying for the past thirty-seven years. In 1983, Hindu revivalist organizations launched a movement for its restoration. On December 19, 1985, a Hindu delegation called on the UP Chief Minister, serving him notice that the temple must be handed over to them by March 8, 1986, otherwise they would forcibly occupy it. On February 11, 1986, the Faizabad district judge ordered the doors of the Babari Mosque, whose case for title is still pending, to be opened so as to let the Hindus exercise their "constitutional right" to worship. A report suggests that the prime minister's cousin, Minister Arun Nahum, "masterminded this coup." (Reported by Neerja Chaudhary in *The Statesman*, New Delhi, April 20, 1986). See *Impact International*, London, June 12-25, 1987; *Muslim India* 53, May 1987.

222. See Rudolph and Rudolph, *In Pursuit of Lakshmi*, pp. 41, 43.

223. Opinion Poll, *India Today*, Oct. 15, 1981, p. 19. This 57% support, if weighted, becomes highly significant, in consideration of the fact that 38% of India's population consists of non-Hindus and untouchable castes.

224. *India Today*, June 15, 1987, pp. 18-9.

225. July 1981, as quoted by Banerjee, p. 62.

226. *New York Times*, August 23, 1981. Ironically, while national political leadership was taking sides, the federal bureaucracy, in general, observed restraint. One example of this difference in style is the *Meenakshipuram Report*, which concludes that there is no available proof of monetary inducement or any other foul play by the Muslim community.

227. *Organiser*, July 19, 1981.

228. Ironically, this letter was addressed to Syed Shahabuddin. "A Muslim Secretary General of the Janata Party," *Muslim India* 14, February 1984.

229. M. V. Kamath, "The Myth of Secularism," in *Indian Express*, October 7, 1983. Also see the *Telegraph*, August 12, 1983. RSS chief BalaSaheb Deoras praised the prime minister for these activities while explaining RSS support of Mrs. Gandhi. Kewal Varma in the *Telegraph*, July 30, 1983.

230. Kudip Nayar in *Current*, August 9, 1986.

231. *Hindu*, March 8, 1982.

232. It was confirmed through a leaked secret note of the Home Ministry, published in the *Statesman*, November 16, 1982 and in *Muslim India* 2, February 1983, p. 89.

233. For details of the episode see *Sunday*, August 30, 1981, p. 27. In my judgment, however, this announcement was one instance of the conversion threats which became popular among untouchables once they saw the magnitude of the response to the Meenakshipuram conversions at the national level. Even without government intervention, conversions in this instance were highly unlikely to occur. The socio-economic milieu in North India, the state of the Muslim and of the untouchable communities there, and most of all the environment of decision in the north, are very different from Tamil Nadu, as I have discussed. Therefore, it is safe to conclude that this announcement of conversion was more a threat to "exit," to seek increased "voice" and more influence in the society, than a serious decision to "resign under protest."

234. Kuldip Nayar reported this meeting between Mrs. Gandhi and the Arya Samaj (a North India-based Hindu revivalist organization) leaders in *Sunday*, August 23, 1981.

235. *Statesman*, November 16, 1982, p. 9. The Madhya Pradesh law, called The Madhya Pradesh Dharma Swatantrya Adhiniyana [Freedom of Religion Act], 1968, prohibits forcible conversions by describing "force" as "...any kind including threat of divine displeasure." It also asks anyone who has taken part in any conversion even indirectly to report it to the district authorities. The validity of these acts was challenged, but they were upheld by the supreme court in *Rev. Stanislaus v. State of Madhya Pradesh* and in *State of Orissa and Others v. Mrs. Yulitha and Others*. The court observed, "It has to be remembered that Article 25(1) [of the Indian Constitution] guarantees 'freedom' of conscience to every citizen, and not merely to the followers of one particular religion, and in turn, postulates that there is no fundamental right to convert another person to one's own religion because if a person purposely undertakes the conversion of another person to his religion, as distinguished from his efforts to transmit or spread the tenets of his religion, that would impinge on the 'freedom of conscience' guaranteed to all the citizens of the country alike." Among other things, the supreme court significantly overlooked the freedom of religion of the person changing his religion or getting converted. For the text of these laws see *Muslim India* 1, January 1983.

236. An image shared by Prime Minister Gandhi but not substantiated by any government investigation or press report, as is discussed in Chapter 9.

237. *Muslim India* 1, January 1983, p. 24. According to the data issued by the Ministry

of Home Affairs, only 7 organizations that received foreign contributions during 1978-79 in Tamil Nadu out of a total of 718 were Muslim. The government has unfortunately not released any data relating the amounts received by these organizations. Lok Sabha Unstarred Question No. 5060, dated March 25, 1981, as published in *Muslim India 7*, July 1983, pp. 296-9.

Chapter 11

238. See Denzil Ibbetson in *Census of Punjab, 1881* 1: Report, Calcutta, 1883; Peter Hardy, "Modern European and Muslim Explanations of Conversion to Islam in South Asia: A Preliminary Survey of the Literature," Journal of the Royal Asiatic Society No. 2, 1977, p. 187.

239. Peter Hardy, "Explanation of Conversion," pp. 185, 186, 190; also see Sheikh M. Ikram, *Ab-e-Kauthar*, (Karachi: Feroze Sons, 1952), pp. 85-6; T. W. Arnold, *The Preaching of Islam*, (Lahore: Shirkat-e-Oualam), pp. 257-97.

240. "Explanation of Conversion," p. 195.

241. Ishtiaq Husain Qureshi, *The Muslim Community of the Indo-Pakistan Subcontinent (610-1947)*, (Karachi: 1977), pp. 1-87.

242. For the crediting of *ulama* see Sayyid Abdul Hasan Ali Nadwi, *Sirat Sayyid Ahmad Shahid*, (Lucknow: 1368 AH), Vol. I pp. 138-40; Vol. II pp. 155-6ff. For the contribution of merchants to the spread of Islam see Syed Sulaiman Nadwi, *Indo-Arab Relations*, Eng. tr., M. Salauddin, (Hyderabad: 1962), pp. 1-53, 243. For the duties of kings, see Ali b. Habib Mawardi, *Ahkam al-Sultaniyah*, 1368 AH, and Imam Ibn Taymiya, *Public Duties in Islam: The Institution of the Hisba*, translated by Muhtar Holland, (Leicester, UK: Islamic Foundation, 1982). For the *Malfuzat* (sufi literature) see Ali ibn Uthman al-Hujwiri, *Kashf almahjub*, trans. Mian Tufail Ahmad, (Lahore: Islamic Publications) and Mohammad Habib, *Hazrat Nizamuddin Auliya: Hayat-o-Ta'limat*, (Delhi: 1972). Dars-e-Nizami is the syllabus taught in all the *madrasas* (Islamic seminaries) of Hanafi schools in South Asia. There is neither a book nor a course dealing with or asking *ulama* to make preaching Islam their primary duty.

244. Quran 22: 77-8. Also see 41: 33-5; 33: 45-6; 2: 143; 5: 8; 2: 140 on the same theme.

245. C. Eric Lincoln, *The Black Muslims in America* (Boston: Beacon Press, 1961), p. 131.

246. Gurr, *Why Men Rebel*, p. 183.

247. Conversion in Tamil Nadu is still going on (Oct. 1987), although the rate of conversion is about 3,000 a year. *Indian Express*, Oct. 30, 1983, reported conversion of 80 untouchables to Islam in Saiyaloor Village of Ramanathapuram District. *Times of India* reported that this is a prelude to the conversion of 3,000 untouchables in ten neighboring villages, as quoted in *Muslim India*, 2 (Jan. 1984):14. The same press report mentioned that 4,000 untouchables had converted to Islam in this district in the previous two years. Untouchable leaders, however, are advising these untouchables to convert in batches without any fanfare. UN 19 Jan. 1984, as quoted in *Muslim India*, 2 (April 1984):157.

248. *India Today*, July 15, 1982; *Sunday*, June 27, 1982.

249. Gurr, *Why Men Rebel*, p. 355.

250. One seminar of untouchable intellectuals and leaders in Maysoor even generally favored and recommended conversion to Islam. A few leftist intellectuals also

favored the decision as a strategic step. For details see: *Radiance*, Delhi, June 8, 1980; *Times of India*, Delhi, March 21, 1981.

Appendix 1

251. Hasan Ali, "Elements of Caste among the Muslims in a District in Southern Bihar," Paratap C. Aggarawal, "Caste Hierarchy in a Meo Village of Rajasthan," Ranjit K. Bhattacharya, "The Concept and Ideology of Caste among the Muslims of Rural Bengal," in *Caste and Social Stratification among Muslims in India*, pp. 22, 142, 293. Also see Mines, *Muslim Merchants* and McGilvray.

252. For a discussion of these trends in the study of caste see: M.N. Srinivas, *Social Change in Modern India* (Berkeley: University of California Press, 1971), pp. 2-6.

253. Also Ghaus Ansari, *Muslim Caste in Utter Pradesh: A Study in Culture Contact* (Lucknow: Ethnographic and Folk Culture Society, 1960); Cora Vreede-de-Steurs, *Parda: A Study of North Indian Muslim Women* (New York: Humanities Press, 1969); A.R. Momin, "Muslim Caste in an Industrial Township of Maharashtra," Aggarwal, "Caste Hierarchy," and Zarina Bhatty, "Status and Power in a Muslim Dominated Village of Utter Pradesh," in *Caste and Social Stratification among Muslims in India*.

254. To check my assumption, I asked fifteen Indian Muslims in Chicago about these words. None of them had heard the word *Ajlaf* before. All, however, were aware of the proper name *Ashraf*, but when asked about the meaning, nine of them said it meant "virtuous" or "pious," "one who does not hurt others," etc. Asked whether they had ever heard this word in reference to Muslim *beraderi* or caste, that this one is *Ashraf* or that one is not, the answer was unanimously "No." *Beraderi*, a term meaning "fraternity," derived from the word for brother commonly used by Muslims in India for clan-size social groups. It is also used sometimes as a Muslim name for caste, as in *sayyad beraderi*.

Appendix 2

255. Louis Dumont, *Homo Hierarchicus: The Caste System and Its Implications* (Chicago: University of Chicago Press, 1980), pp. 214-5.

256. Eleanor Mae Zelliot, "Dr. Ambedkar and the Mahar Movement," (Ph.D. dissertation, University of Pennsylvania, 1969), p. 222.

257. Keer, p. 270.

258. Jervis, p. 32.

259. V.T. Rajshekar Shetty, "Ambedkar and His Conversion: A Critique," (Bangalore: Dalit Action Committee, Karnalaka), p. 10.

Appendix 3

260. Dr. Mumtaz Ali Khan, *A Brief Summary of the Study on "Mass Conversions of Meenakshipuram: a Sociological Enquiry"*, in typescript.

Glossary of Selected
Terms and Names

ADMK   Anna Dravida Munnetra Kazhagam, a faction of DMK (Dravida Munnetra Kazhagam), is a Tamil nationalist political party named after its charismatic leader Anna Durai.

Adi Dravida or
Adi-Dravidians   A Tamil term for untouchables, meaning the "original dravidians." Dravidian is the race Tamils belong to. This term connotes the origins of the untouchables as those subjected by Aryan invaders. A substantial number of Tamil untouchables declare themselves as Adi Dravida in the census, instead of by their caste name.

baboo (or babu)   Loosely, persons with low paid white collar jobs and a working knowledge of English. It is a form of address usually used by illiterate common people in India.

backward classes (or backward castes)   A term loosely applied to the Shudra castes in India, that is, those above untouchables but below the twice-born castes of Brahmins, Kshatriyas, and Vaisyas.

Brahmins   The priestly caste in India, at the top of the caste hierarchy.

DMK   Dravida Munnetra Kazhagam (Dravidian Progressive Federation), the first political party promoting Tamil nationalism in accordance with the ideology of Ramaswami Naicker. It was founded by Anna Durai.

Dalit Panthers   An untouchables' militant organization.

dharma   The sacred and traditional prescription of Hindu life describing the rules and prohibitions of such activities as interdining and intermarriage, deviation from which can invite punishment from caste council or the dominant caste in that area.

Dravida Kazhagam   The main Tamil nationalist party established in 1944 by Ramaswami Naicker. Later its message was carried on by its factions, the Dravida Munnetra Kazhagam (DMK, Dravidian Progressive Federation), ADMK, and AIADMK.

Dravida Nadu   Land of the dravidian people. It was Dravidian Movement's demand that four southern Indian states where dravidians live be declared a sovereign Dravida Nadu. Madras was eventually renamed Tamil Nadu as a result of a scaled down version of this demand.

dravidian   A member of the dravidian race.

dwija   Literally twice-born. The three high castes, Brahmins, Kshatriyas, and Vaisyas, are considered twice-born in Hinduism, and have such privileges as studying religious scriptures.

Eid   Two of the most important Muslim festivals, one called Eid ul Fitr comes at the end of the fasting month of Ramadan. The other, called Eid ul Adha, comes at the end of Haj (pilgrimage) in commemoration of the prophet Abraham's jihad and sacrifice. Muslims spend the most on these holidays.

Ezhavas   An untouchable caste in the South Indian state of Kerala.

fiqh   Literally "understanding" or "comprehension" in Arabic, the discipline of Islamic jurisprudence.

hanafi   One of the five schools of Islamic jurisprudence, named after its scholar, Abu Hanifa (AD 699-767).

harijan   Literally "son of Hari" (a Hindu god). Another name for untouchables, given to them by Gandhi with the intention of remedying their position of lowest in the social hierarchy. Harijan is the most frequently used term for untouchables in the Indian heartland. Many educated untouchables and their leaders, however, dislike the term. Dr. Ambedkar asked untouchables not to use it.

hundy   Illegal and extra-legal transactions of money in and out of India, across the national boundaries.

imam   An Islamic prayer leader. In its common usage it is not a position in any type of clerical hierarchy. As a title, it is used for any great Islamic scholar, such as Abu Hanifa and Al Shafei among the Sunnis. The Shi'a use the term for the leader of the community in the succession of the prophet Muhammad.

jati   Indian name for caste which is generally translated as "sub-caste" in English.

juma khutba   Sermon delivered in mosques before Friday afternoon congregational prayer.

kalima   *Kalima, Shahadah*, or *Kalima-e-Shahadat*, the declaration of belief in Islam: "I declare that there is no god but God, He is One and has no partner. And I also declare that Muhammad is His servant and His Messenger." In short, *"La Ilaha illal Lah, Muhammad ur Rasoolul Lah"* (There is no god but God, and Muhammad is the messenger of God). In South Asia the shorter version is called Kalima; the longer version is called Kalima-e-Shahadat.

Kayalar   A group name of Tamil Muslims, not equivalent to caste, and rarely used.

Kerala   State in southwest India, bordering Tamil Nadu.

khilafat   Caliphate, literally "successor" in Arabic. Khalifa is a Quranic title given to Adam (Quran 2:30) and, by extension to all mankind. In history, *khalifa* became the title of the successors of the prophet Muhammad, notably the first four Rightly-Guided Caliphs (AD 632-655).

Khilafat Movement   Although with the establishment of Umayyad hereditary rule (AD 655) the institution of Khilafat changed into monarchy, Muslim rulers kept calling themselves Caliphs. When Turkey (of the Ottoman Caliphate) was under Allied threat, Muslims in India launched a protest movement against the British-named Khilafat Movement (1919-1924).

Kshatriyas   The second caste in the caste hierarchy, after Brahmins.

kuti   Matri-clan.

Labbai   Term sometimes used for Tamil-speaking Muslims.

Madhya Pradesh   State in central India.

madrasa   An Islamic seminary.

Mahar   An untouchable caste in the Indian state of Maharashtra. Dr. Ambedkar—the most prominent untouchable leader—was from this caste. Mahars converted to Buddhism en masse along with Dr. Ambedkar.

Maharashtra   A southern Indian state.

Malabar   Historical name for the coastal areas of the South Indian state of Kerala.

Manu   Book of Hindu laws.

Marakayar   Rarely used name for a group of Tamil Muslims.

maulavi   Title applied to a prayer leader or a Muslim religious scholar in South Asia.

Mughal   (mogul) One of the chain of Muslim dynasties in India founded by Babur (1483-1530). Although the Great Mughals ended with Aurangzeb (1658-1707), the dynasty continued nominally until 1857.

Musalman   In South Asia and Iran, a Muslim.

NWFP   North West Frontier Province of Pakistan, commonly referred to by Pakistanis as Sarhad.

Nadars   An untouchable caste in Tamil Nadu.

Naxalite   Name derived from "Nexal Bari," the stronghold of a Leninist-Marxist faction of the Communist Party in the Indian state of West Bengal which opted for violent struggle to liberate the peasantry there. Later, this name was mainly used by law enforcement agencies and landlords to legitimize their excesses against any rural mobilization of the rural classes, in Bihar, UP, and Tamil Nadu in the eighties.

Neo-Buddhists   Those untouchables who converted to Buddhism in the late fifties in Dr. Ambedkar's conversion movement, mainly in Maharashtra and predominantly from the Mahar caste.

PCR   Protection of Civil Rights Act.

Paraiyar   The largest untouchable caste in Tamil Nadu. The English word "pariah" is a derivative of this name.

qiyas   Rational analogy, one of the four principles of Islamic jurisprudence.

RSS   Rashtriya Swayamsevak Sangh—one of the most important Hindu revivalist organizations with a fascist style and program. One of its members killed Gandhi.

Ramayana   The most popular story in Hindu mythology, in which Rama (a northern Aryan king) defeats Ravana (a southern Dravidian king).

Rawthers   Name of a social stratum of Tamil Muslims, rarely used.

reservations   Seats and quotas reserved for some socially backward group in educational institutions, government services.

sanskritization   Tendency of the lower castes to imitate the social and ritualistic practices of the higher castes.

satyagraha   non-violent, but unconstitutional, civil disobedience.

scheduled castes   Official term for untouchables. This term was adopted in 1935, when the British listed the untouchable castes in a schedule appended to the Government of India Act for the purpose of statutory safeguards and other benefits. Later, the Constitution of India 1950, article 366, section 24, adopted the same usage.

shafei　　Muslims following the Shafei school of Islamic jurisprudence, ascribed to al-Shafei (767-820).

Shahadat e Haq　　"Being witness to the truth," term based on Quranic words coined by the Pakistan's Islamic leader Mawdidi. The term means that it is the duty of each Muslim to be witness to Islam by his/her words and deeds.

shuddhi　　"purifying" in Sanskrit, a term used by Hindu chauvinist organizations to describe their reconversion efforts.

Shudras　　The fourth and the largest (at the bottom of caste hierarchy, just above untouchables) caste of the ideal Hindu social order, varna.

sunnah　　The reported traditions and sayings of the prophet Muhammad. It is the second source of Islamic law after Quran.

taleef-al-koloob　　A derivative of the Quranic words meaning "those whose hearts have been recently reconciled." Financial help to a new Muslim is one of the designated usages of Zakat in Quran.

taluka　　An administrative subdivision of a district.

Tamilian　　Tamil-speaking person, a Tamil.

tawhid　　"A relationship with the Only One (God) that excludes a similar relationship with any one else." Tawhid is the single most important belief, term, and concept in Islam.

Thakur　　A land-owning dominant caste in northern Indian.

Thevars　　A land-owning low caste in Tamil Nadu, ritually just above the untouchables.

Turukudu　　Derived from "Turk," conveying an image of foreigner and invader, used as a derogative for Muslims in Tamil.

UOA　　Untouchability (Offense) Act of India 1955.

ulema　　Plural of "alim," Muslim scholars of the Islamic law and religion.

ummah　　People, community, or (literally) nation, the term used by Muslims all over the world about themselves as one people, connoting the brotherhood of the faithful.

untouchability   The discriminating and racist customs, practices, and behavior of non-untouchable castes towards untouchables. It can be traditional treatment sanctioned by the Brahminic laws and Hindu tradition or it can be discrimination based upon their social position.

Urdu   A South Asian language of Indo-Aryan family, written in Arabic script, the lingua franca of Pakistanis and Indian Muslims. Muslims of British India considered it their cultural language. It is Pakistan's national language. Its usage as a medium of education constitute a regular demand of Indian Muslims today.

Uttar Pradesh   The most populated northern state of India.

Vaisyas   The third, trader, class in the Hindu caste system (varna).

varna   Usually translated "caste," literally "color," the classical division of Hindu society. There are four varnas: Brahmins, Kshatriyas, Vaisyas, and Shudras. Untouchables are considered outside this system, thus avarna, i.e., out-caste.

Vishva Hindu Parishad   An alliance of Hindu revivalist organizations in India, leading the current wave of Hindu revivalism.

yatras   Pilgrimages, ritual visits to Hindu sacred places. Hindu revivalists use this term for religious processions in India today.

zakat   Purification and growth in Arabic, a compulsory monetary contribution paid yearly by every Muslim possessing more than a certain amount of wealth and property. Zakat is the third pillar of Islam. Every Muslim is supposed to pay it to Islamic government, or in its absence to the poor and distressed.

Bibliography

Books

Aggarawal, Paratap C. "Caste Hierarchy in a Meo Village of Rajasthan," in *Caste and Social Stratification among Muslims in India*. pp. 141-158, ed. Imtiaz Ahmad, New Delhi: Manohar, 1978.

Ahmad, Imtiaz, ed. *Caste and Social Stratification among Muslims in India*. New Delhi: Manohar, 1978.

Ahir, D.C. *Buddhism and Ambedkar*. New Delhi: Ajay Parkashan, 1968.

Ali, Hasan, "Elements of Caste among the Muslims in a District in Southern Bihar," in *Caste and Social Stratification among Muslims in India*, pp. 19-40, ed. Imtiaz Ahmad. New Delhi: Manohar, 1978.

Ansari, Ghous. *Muslim Caste in Utter Pradesh: A Study in Culture Conflict*. Lucknow: Ethnographic and Folk Culture Society, 1960.

Arnold, David. *The Congress in Tamil Nadu: Nationalist Politics in South India, 1919-1937*. New Delhi: Manohar, 1977.

Arnold, T.W. *The Congress in Tamil Nadu: Nationalist Politics in South India, 1919-1937*. New Delhi: Manohar, 1977.

Baker, J. Christopher. *The Politics of South India, 1920-1937*. Cambridge: Cambridge University Press, 1976.

Banerjee, B. Nath. *Religious Conversion in India*. New Delhi, 1982.

Barnett, Marguerite Ross. *The Politics of Cultural Nationalism in South India*. Princeton: Princeton University Press, 1976.

Beteille, Andre. *Caste, Class, and Power: Changing Patterns of Stratification in a Tanjor Village*. Berkeley: University of California Press, 1965.

Bharatia Janata Party. *The Meenakshipuram Report*, issued by Headquarters General Secretary Tamil Nadu BJP, n.d.

Bhattacharya, Ranjit K. "The Concept and Ideology of Caste among the Muslims of Rural Bengal." in *Caste and Social Stratification among Muslims in India*, pp. 269-298, ed. Imtiaz Ahmad. New Delhi: Manohar, 1978.

Bhatty, Zarina. "Status and Power in a Muslim Dominated Village of Utter Pradesh," in *Caste and Social Stratification among Muslims in India*, pp. 207-224, ed. Imtiaz Ahmad, New Delhi: Manohar, 1978.

Bienen, Henry. *Violence and Social Change: A Review of Current Literature*. Chicago: University of Chicago Press, 1968.

Davies James C., "Towards a Theory of Revolution," in *Anger, Violence, and Politics: Theories and Research*. pp. 58-66, ed. Ivo I. Feierabend, Rosalind L. Feierabend, and Ted R. Gurr. Englewood Cliffs, N.J.: Prentice-Hall, 1972.

Diehl, Anita. *E.V. Ramaswami Naiker-Periyar: A Study of the Influence of a Personality in Contemporary South India*. Stockholm: Esselte Studium, 1977.

Dumont, Louis. *Homo Hierarchichus: The Caste System and Its Implications*. Chicago: University of Chicago Press, 1980.

Feierabend, Ivo K., Feierabend, Rosalind L. and Nesvold, Betty A. "Social Change and Political Violence: Cross National Patterns." in *Anger, Violence, and Politics: Theories and Research*. pp. 107-124, ed. Ivo K. Feierabend, Rosalind L. Feierabend and Ted R. Gurr. Englewood Cliffs, N.J.: Prentice-Hall, 1972.

Fernandes, Walter. *Caste and Conversion Movements in India: Religion and Human Rights*. New Delhi: Indian Social Institute, 1981.

Friedmann, Y., "A Contribution to the Early History of Islam in India." in *Studies in Memory of Gaston Wiet*, pp. 309-333. ed. Mariam Rosen-Ayalon. Jerusalem: Institute of Asian and African Studies, The Hebrew University of Jerusalem, 1977.

Galanter, Marc. *Competing Equalities: Law and the Backward Classes in India*. Berkeley: University of California press, 1984.

Gough, E. Kathleen. "The Social Structure of a Tanjore Village." in *Village India: Studies in the Little Community*, pp. 36-52. ed. McKim Marriott. Chicago: University of Chicago Press, 1955.

Gupta, Giri Raj, ed. "Changing Caste Attitudes towards Harijans" in *Cohesion and Conflict in Modern India*. Durham, 1978.

Gurr, Robert Ted. "Psychological Factors in Civil Violence." in *Anger, Violence, and Politics*, pp. 31-57. ed. Iva K. Feierabend, Rosalind L. Feierabend, and Ted R. Gurr. Englewood Cliffs, N.J.: Prentice-Hall, 1972.

_____. *Why Men Rebel*. Princeton: Princeton University Press, 1977.

Hardgrave, Jr., Robert L. *The Dravidian Movement*. Bombay: Popular Prakashan, 1965.

_____. *The Nadars of Tamil Nadu: The Political Culture of a Community in Change*. Berkeley: University of California Press, 1969.

_____. *Essays in the Political Sociology of South India*. Delhi: Usha Publications, 1979.

_____. *India: Government and Politics in a Developing Nation*. New York, 1980.

Hardy, P. *The Muslims of British India*. Cambridge: Cambridge University Press, 1972.

Hirschman, Albert O. *Exit, Voice and Loyalty: Responses to Decline in Firms, Organizations, and States*. Cambridge: Harvard University Press, 1970.

Huntington, Samuel P. *Political Order in Changing Societies*. New Haven: Yale University Press, 1968.

Hutton, J.H. *Caste in India: Its Nature, Function, and Origins*. Cambridge: Cambridge University Press, 1946.

Jervis, Robert. *Perception and Misperception in International Politics*, Princeton: Princeton University Press, 1976.

Joshi, Barbara. *Democracy in Search of Equality: Untouchable Politics and Indian Social Change*. Delhi: Hindustan Publishing Corporation, 1982.

Juergensmeyer, Mark. *Religion as Social Vision: The Movement against Untouchability in 20th-Century Punjab*. Berkeley: University of California Press, 1982.

Keer, Dhananjay. *Dr. Ambedkar: Life and Mission*. Bombay: Popular Prakashan, 1962.

Khan, Mohammad Raza. "Origin and Growth of Muslim Colleges in the South," in *Tamil Nadu Muslim Educational Conference, 1973, Souvenir*. Madras: Tamil Nadu Muslim Education Standing Committee, 1973 (no page numbers given, n.d.).

Kulke, Eckehard, "Integration, Alienation and Rejection: The Status of 'Untouchables'." in *Aspects of Changing India*, pp. 244-254. ed. S. Devadas Pillai. Bombay: Popular Prakashan, 1976.

Lindsay, Peter H. and Norman, Donald A. *Human Information Processing: An Introduction to Psychology*. New York: Academic Press, 1972.

Lincoln, C. Eric. *The Black Muslims in America*. Boston: Beacon Press, 1961.

Mencher, P. Joan. "Continuity and Change in an Ex-untouchable Community of South India." in *Untouchables in Contemporary India*, pp. 37-56. ed. J. Michael Mahar. Tucson, Arizona: University of Arizona Press, 1972.

Merton, Robert K. *Social Theory and Social Structure*. New York: Free Press, 1963.

Mines, Mattison. *Muslim Merchants: The Economic Behaviour of an Indian Muslim Community*. New Delhi: Shri Ram Centre for Industrial Relations and Human Resources, 1972.

_____. "Social Stratification among Muslim Tamils in Tamil Nadu, South India," in *Caste and Social Stratification among Muslims in India*, pp. 159-170. ed. Imtiaz Ahmad. New Delhi: Manohar, 1978.

Momin, A.R. "Muslim Caste in an Industrial Township of Maharashtra," in *Caste and Social Stratification among Muslims in India*, pp. 117-140. ed. Imtiaz Ahmad. New Delhi: Manohar, 1978.

Naidu, Ratna. *Communal Edge to Plural Societies*. New Delhi: Vicas, 1980.

Nieburg, H.L. *Political Violence: The Behavioral Process*. New York: St. Martin's Press, 1969.

Rajshekar Shetty, V.T. *Ambedkar and His Conversion: A Critique*. Bangalore: Dalit Action Committee Karnataka, 1980.

Redfield, Robert. *The Little Community*. Chicago: University of Chicago Press, 1955.

Rose, Arnold M. *The Negro's Morale: Group Identification and Protest*. Minneapolis: University of Minnesota Press, 1949.

_____.*Assuring Freedom to the Free: A Century of Emancipation in the U.S.A.* with an introduction by Lyndon B. Johnson. Detroit: Wayne State University Press, 1964.

Rudolph, Lloyd I. and Rudolph, Susanne Hoeber. *The Modernity of Tradition: Political Development in India*. Chicago: University of Chicago Press, 1967.

_____. *In Pursuit of Lakshmi: The Political Economy of the Indian State*. Chicago: University of Chicago Press,1987

_____. "Determinants and Varieties of Agrarian Mobilization," in *Agrarian Power and Agrigarian Productivity in South Asia.* ed. Meghnad Desai, Susanne H. Rudolph, and Ashok Rudra, Delhi: Oxford University Press.

Saraswathi, S. *Minorities in Madras State: Group Interest in Modern Politics.* Delhi: Impex India, 1974.

Siddiqi, Muhammad Nejatullah. *Issues in Islamic Banking: Selected Papers.* Leicester, UK: Islamic Foundation,1983.

Siddiqui, M.K.A. "Caste among the Muslims of Calcutta." in *Caste and Social Stratification among Muslims in India*, pp. 243-268. ed. Imtiaz Ahmad, New Delhi: Manohar, 1978.

Srinivas, M.N. *Social Change in Modern India*, Berkeley: University of California Press, 1971.

Srinivasa Aiyangar, M. *Tamil Studies: or Essays on the History of the Tamil People, Language, Religion and Literature*, First Series. Madras: Guardian Press, 1914.

Sulaiman, S.M. and Ismail, M.M. *Islam, Indian Religions and Tamil Culture.* ed. Devasenapathi. Madras: University of Madras Press, 1977.

"A Survey of Muslim Education in Tamil Nadu," in *Tamil Nadu Muslim Educational Conference 1973, Souvenir.* Madras.

Tocqueville, Alexis de. *The Old Regime and the French Revolution.* trans. Stuart Gilbert, Garden City, N.Y.: Doubleday and Company, 1955.

Vreede-de-Steurs, Cora. *Parda: A Study of North Indian Muslim Women.* New York: Humanities Press, 1969.

Weiner, Myron. "Political Participation: Crisis of the Political Process." in *Crises and Sequences in Political Development*, pp. 159-204. ed. Leonard Binder et al., Princeton: Princeton University Press, 1971.

Zimmerman, Ekkart. *Political Violence, Crises and Revolutions: Theories and Research.* Cambridge, Mass.: Schenkman Publishing Co., 1983.

Articles

Alvares, Claude. "Tamil Nadu's Police State," in *Indian Express* magazine, Jan. 10, 1982, pp. 1,4.

Anderson, Walter K. "India in 1981: Stronger Political Authority and Social Tension." *Asian Survey* MKII (Feb. 1982): 119-135.

Bhide, Amar. "India's Conflict between Dirigism and Democracy," *Wall Street Journal.* May 17, 1982, p. 27.

Brass, Paul. "Uttar Pradesh," *State Politics in India.* Princeton, 1968, p. 96.

Chopra, O.P. "Unaccounted Income: Some Estimates," *Economic and Political Weekly.* May 1, 1982, pp. 739-744.

Dutt, Dev. "Conversions," *Seminar 269.* (Jan. 1982), pp. 41-45.

Elliott, Gregory C. "Components of Pacifism: Conceptualization and Measurement." *Journal of Conflict Resolution.* 24 (March 1980): 27-54.

Grimshaw, Allen D. "Interpreting Collective Violence: An argument for the Importance of Social Structure." *Annals of the AAPSS.* 391 (Sept. 1970), pp. 9-20.

Gupta, Poonam and Gupta, Sanjeev. "Estimates of the Unreported Economy in India." *Economic and Political Weekly.* Jan. 16, 1982, pp. 70-75.

Hardy, Peter. "Modern European and Muslim Explanations of Conversion to Islam in South Asia: A Preliminary Survey of the Literature." *Journal of the Royal Asiatic Society.* No. 2, 1977, pp. 177-206.

Harriss, John, "Why Poor People Stay Poor in Rural South India," *Social Scientist.* 8 (Aug. 1979): 20-47.

Heirich, Max. "Change of Heart: A Test of Some Widely Held Theories about Religious Conversion." *American Journal of Sociology.* 83: 653-680.

Joshi, Barbara R. "Whose Law, Whose Order: Untouchables, Social Violence and the State in India," *Asian Survey.* XXII (July 1982): 676-687.

Khan, Mumtaz Ali. "A Brief Summary of the Study on 'Mass Conversions of Meenakshipuram: A Sociological Enquiry.' " *Religion and Society.* XXVII (Dec. 1981): 37-50.

Lal, Sheo Kumar. "Occupational Aspiration of Scheduled Caste Students," *Social Change.* 6 (March-June 1976): 26-32.

Mathew, George. "Politicisation of Religion: Conversion to Islam in Tamil Nadu." *Economic and Political Weekly.* June 19 & 26, 1982.

Mukarji, Nirmal. "The Hindu Problem," *Seminar 269* (Jan. 1982).

Naidu, Usha S. "Socialisation of Scheduled Caste Children at School." *Social Change.* Delhi, Dec. 1979.

Nieburg, H.L. "The Threat of Violence and Social Change." *American Political Science Review.* LVI (Dec. 1962): 865-873.

Raj, Albones S. "Mass Religious Conversion as Protest Movement: A Framework." *Religion and Society*. XXV III (Dec. 1981): 58-66.

Rudolph, Lloyd I. "Urban Life and Populist Radicalism: Dravidian Politics in Madras," *The Journal of Asian Studies*. XX (May 1961): 283-297.

Rudolph, Lloyd I. and Rudolph, Susanne Hoeber. "Rethinking Secularism: Genesis and Implications of the Textbook Controversy, 1977-79." *Pacific Affairs*. 56 (Spring 1983): 15-37.

Sharma, S.L. "Conversions." *Seminar*. 268 (Dec. 1981), pp. 27-34.

Shourie, Arun. "Reasons for Hope." *New Quest*. (July-Aug. 1983).

Tharamangalam, Joseph. "The Communist Movement and the Theory and Practice of Peasant Mobilization in India." *Journal of Contemporary Asia*. II, No. 4 (1981).

Turk, Austin T. "Social Dynamics of Terrorism." *Annals of the AAPSS*. 463 (Sept. 1982), pp. 119-128.

Turner, J.B. Gokhale. "Bhakti or Viroda." *Journal of Asian and African Studies*. XV , 1-2 (1980).

Weiner, Myron. "International Migration and Development: Indians in the Persian Gulf." *Population and Development Review*. 8 (March 1982): I-36.

Wingate, Andrew. "A Study of Conversion from Christianity to Islam in Two Tamil Villages." *Religion and Society*. XXVIII (Dec. 1981): 3-36.

Wright, Jr., Theodore P. "The Muslim League in South India since Independence: A Study in Minority Group Political Strategies," *American Political Science Review*. LK (1966): 579-599.

Yagnik, Achyut and Bhatt, Anil. "The Anti-Dalit Agitation in Gujarat." *South Asia Bulletin*. IV:1, Spring 1984, pp. 45-60.

Indian Government Publications

Census of India, 1971 Series 1-India, *Polygynous Marriages in India Survey*, Miscellaneous Studies. Monograph No. 4 (1961 series).

Census of India 1971, Series 1, India, part II-C(i). *Social and Cultural Tables*. Delhi: Controller of Publications, 1979.

Census of India 1981, Series 1, India. Paper 1 of 1981. *Provisional Population Tables*. New Delhi: Registrar General and Census Commissioner, 1981.

Census of India 1981, Series 1, India. Paper 2 of 1981. *Provisional Population Tables: Rural-Urban Distribution.* New Delhi: Registrar General and Census Commissioner, 1981.

Census of India 1971, Series 19, Tamil Nadu. Part II-A. *General Population Tables.* Delhi: Controller of Publications, 1972.

Census of India 1971, Series 19, Tamil Nadu. Part II-B(i). *General Economic Tables.* Delhi: Controller of Publications, 1976.

Census of India 1971, Series 19, Tamil Nadu. Part II-C-(i). *Social and Cultural Tables.* Delhi: Controller of Publications, 1978.

Census of India 1971, Series 19, Tamil Nadu. Part X-B. *District Census Handbook, Maduri District,* Vol. II. Madras: Director of Stationery and Printing, 1972.

Census of India 1971, Series 19, Tamil Nadu. Part X-B, *District Census Handbook, Ramanathapuram District.* Vol. 1. Madras: Director of Publications and Printing, 1972.

Central Statistical Organisation, *Statistical Abstract India 1978,* New Series No. 23 (n.d.)

Office of the Commissioner for Scheduled Castes and Scheduled Tribes, *Report of the Commissioner for Scheduled Castes and Scheduled Tribes 1977-78.* 2 parts. Delhi: Controller of Publications, 1979.

_____. *Report of the Commissioner for Scheduled Castes and Scheduled Tribes 1978-79,* 2 parts. Delhi: Controller of Publications, 1980.

_____. Madras. *The Meenakshipuram Report,* as published in *Sunday,* Nov. 7-13, 1982.

Ministry of Information and Broadcasting. *Social Background of India's Administrators: A Socio-Economic Study of the Higher Civil Services of India,* by V. Subramaniam. New Delhi: Publication Division, 1971.

_____. *A Reference Annual 1980.* New Delhi: Publication Division, 1980.

Ministry of Law, Justice and Company Affairs. *The Constitution of India* (as modified up to August 1, 1977). Delhi: Controller of Publications, 1978.

Report of the Backward Classes Commission: Tamil Nadu, 1970. 3 vol. Madras: Director of Stationery and Printing, 1974.

Report of the Backward Classes Commission 1980, 2 parts. Delhi: Controller of Publications, 1981.

Unpublished Material

Ahmad, Imtiaz. "The Tamilnadu Conversion, Conversion Threats and the Anti-Reservation Campaign: Some Hypotheses" (typewritten ms.).

Bouton, Marshall M. "The Sources of Agrarian Radicalism: A Study of Thanjavur District, South India," Ph.D. dissertation, University of Chicago, 1979.

Fussell, Jerome J. "Muslims' Methods of Propagating the Faith." M.A. thesis, University of Chicago, 1949.

Kananaikil, Jose. "Reaching Inward from the Periphery," Ph.D. dissertation, University of Chicago, 1981.

Malik, Abdul. "Monthly Massacres of Untouchables." (Course paper, Department of Political Science, University of Chicago, 1982, typescript).

McGilvray, Dennis B. "Tamils and Moors: Caste and Matriclan Structure in Eastern Sri Lanka," Ph.D. dissertation, University of Chicago, 1974.

Mitchell, Nora. "Cultural Homogeneity in Tamil Nadu." M.A. thesis, University of Chicago, 1963.

Siraj, Maqbool. "Conversion in Tamil Nadu, 1980" (typewritten ms.).

Zelliot, Eleanor Mae, "Dr. Ambedkar and the Mahar Movement," Ph.D. dissertation, University of Pennsylvania, 1968.

Index

and untouchables, 1, 2
census data, 11
communal riots, 77, 88
denial of caste among, 109
ex-Mughal complex, 2
identity and interests of, 5
in Indian history textbooks, 91
in services, compared with untouchables, 21
loss of elites, 2
perceptions of powerlessness, 70
polygyny and, 132n.204
regional comparison of, 60-61, 65-66, 77, 90
regional nationalism and, 2
revivalist tendencies among, 87, 90
studies of Muslim social behavior, 110
Muslims in Tamil Nadu, 9
absence of caste among, 67-69
as compared to North, 60-61, 65-67, 70
communal polarization and, 77
contacts with untouchables, 58
history of, 61, 132n.200
political position of, 55, 69-70
revivalist tendencies among, 62, 71
socio-economic position of, 63, 64-65
support of Dravidian nationalism, 62, 69, 76

Nadars, (see caste names)
Naicker, Periyar E.V. Ramaswami, 4, 27, 73, 75, 76, 77
Narainaswamy, Guru, 4
Naxalites, 9, 33, 36, 37, 80, 81-82, 105-107
Nehru, Jawahir Lal, 98
Neo-buddhists, 33, 85-86, 104 (also see Buddhism)
Nepal, 88
New Delhi, 94
New York Times, The, 87
Nieburg, H.L., 14, 92
Nizams of Hyderabad, 61
North West Frontier Province (NWFP), 60

Organiser, 87
Orissa, 98

Pakistan, 60, 64, 70, 76, 91
Panchayat, 43
Pandya, 61
Persian Gulf, 87
Police, 30, 44, 53-54, 81-82
Prachur, 34
Protection of Civil Right Act, 24, 53
Psychological violence, 8, 106
Puliangudi riots, 95

Qiyas, 61
Quran
as source of Islamic law, 61
business of Tamil Muslims and, 62
model of inter-group relations in, 78
Muslims' duty of being witness before mankind, 103
recipients of zakat, 127n.132
zakat-welfare due in, 64, 127n.131
Qureshi, Prof. Ishtiaq, 101, 102
Qutabshahi, 61

RSS (Rashtriya Swayamsevak Sangh), 62, 86, 97
Rahman, Abdur M.W., 70
Rai, Lajpat, 77
Rajarajeshwari Tripurasundari temple, 97
Rajasthan, 96
Ram, Jagjivan, 37, 107
Ramanathapuram temple, 51
Ramanathapuram, 36, 42, 47
Ramayana, 75
Ramjanmabhoomi temple, 5
Reconversion movement, 95-96
Reference group theory, 42
Relative deprivation, 3, 11, 12, 42, 45, 52-53, 104-105
Report on Backward Classes, Tamil Nadu, 64
Rifaee, A.K., 70
Riots
backward classes vs. untouchables, 41
Hindu revivalists vs. Christians, 95
Hindu vs. Muslims, 77
reasons for, 41
untouchable vs. higher castes, 27, 32-33, 34, 35-36, 86
Rising expectations, 3, 12